ROBER

AWAKEN AND COME ALIVE!

The Power of Self-Awareness

Featuring

The 5 Master Keys For Life Success

outskirts
press

Awaken and Come Alive!
The Power of Self-Awareness Featuring The 5 Master Keys For Life Success
All Rights Reserved.
Copyright © 2021 Robert Hernandez
v5.0

The opinions expressed in this manuscript are solely the opinions of the author and do not represent the opinions or thoughts of the publisher. The author has represented and warranted full ownership and/or legal right to publish all the materials in this book.

This book may not be reproduced, transmitted, or stored in whole or in part by any means, including graphic, electronic, or mechanical without the express written consent of the publisher except in the case of brief quotations embodied in critical articles and reviews.

Outskirts Press, Inc.
http://www.outskirtspress.com

ISBN: 978-1-9772-3468-1

Cover Photo © 2021 www.gettyimages.com. All rights reserved - used with permission.

Outskirts Press and the "OP" logo are trademarks belonging to Outskirts Press, Inc.

PRINTED IN THE UNITED STATES OF AMERICA

This book is dedicated to my Mom.
You lived at a higher level, close to God.
You are Love. You are Light.
We Love you.

"Awaken and Come Alive" is a well written and well-thought of book that touches the fibers of family, life and relationships. Drawn from real life experiences, it speaks of compassion, understanding and overcoming adversities. There is a heart-warming blend of poignancy and inspiration. Robert Hernandez articulated brilliance and sensitivity. Each concept shared is a lesson learned. This is one, if not the best motivational manuscripts I have ever read.

Mel Christopher Magboo, MD
Geriatrician
Co-founder, Geriatric Specialty Care
Palliative Medicine/Hospice Medical Director

Awaken and Come Alive by Robert Hernandez is a must-read book that reveals a clear path to understanding self-awareness, a book that also reveals ways and methods to awaken your life with new perspectives. Today, everyone is looking for clues and hints that spark new and creative realities that lead to a better, more productive life. Note this simple but key master point--"The more one discovers about oneself, the more challenges, perspectives, and opportunities unfold."

Throughout Hernandez's book are numerous historical analogies that help clarify the world we live in. For example, "Pythagoras saw patterns of truth above at the universal level ... "After all,' Hernandez writes, "anything that holds up the universe surely can be put to good use to uphold our lives."

Grab this inspirational book, sit back, get comfortable, and enjoy the journey.

Hugh Fraser M.A
Novelist and Professor of English

As I read, "Awaken and Come Alive," I was inspired at the wisdom behind the words of Robert Hernandez. Embrace his concepts and insights. Make a conscious choice to improve your relationship with your own thoughts for they will assist you in coming awake and being alive. This book is your friend. Hold it close.

Larry James, author of "How to
Really Love the One You're With."

Well-written and timely! The stories and questions for introspection are compelling and revealing. A must-read for anyone interested in creating and manifesting a game-changing life.

Phil Johncock, Co-Author of
The Power of Creativity &
Co-Creator of the Creativity Hub

Table of Contents

Introduction: The Way Out Is In i

Section I. Master Invisible Forces

Chapter One: You're It!... 7

Chapter Two: Focus your Attention 13

Chapter Three: Shape your Attitude............................ 20

Chapter Four: Strengthen the Will 29

Chapter Five: Manage Your Emotions 33

Chapter Six: Change your Beliefs 39

Section II. Master Order

Chapter Seven: Holding Patterns................................. 61

Section III. Master Creativity

Chapter Eight: FYI !... 81

Section IV. Master Change

Chapter Nine: A New Change is in Order................... 91

Section V. Master Relationship

Chapter Ten: The Relationship Connection 102

Conclusion: Re-Tooling the Master Craftsman 113

References 118

INTRODUCTION
The Way Out Is In

A path lies ahead, but within as we find our way by the light of understanding.

Imagine setting foot on uncharted territory. The land is fertile and untouched, where no one has treaded before. Ahead lies a lush thick forest that draws your attention. The forest beauty is captivating, but what lies within is a mystery unseen. You take the first step forward to the unknown. For a short while the way is clear with nothing to deter or fear. As you enter the woods, darkness begins to surround you. The feeling of being lost overcomes you with the question: Which way do I go? Fear sets in, but so does a sense of survival!

As you scan the dark forest, your eyes are drawn to a beam of sunlight in the distance that has found its way through the thick trees, illuminating a most tranquil setting. Your inclination is to go to the light as it serves as a beckon to a safe and peaceful haven, a bright spot ahead. Yet, there is hesitancy as another part of you wants to turn back to the way of the known, the past path. Do I turn around or straight ahead! Who will win before you begin?

The Right Fight

The human potential is extraordinary beyond measure. Amazingly, in a relatively short period of time, man has discovered fire, invented the wheel, and touched the surface of the moon. We went forward by setting foot and mind on unchartered territory, as we connected our country by way of the inter-continental railroad, and more recently the world through the Internet. From rail line to on-line, nothing on earth should dominate the human potential.

While we have demonstrated control over the external, our inner domain for self-control remains a challenge. While our most powerful resources are within, so too is our most daunting opponent who desires to override the landscape of our minds like ancient horsemen running rampant, pillaging, and conquering more of our interior states of mind. I know, it sounds like Genghis Khan and a pack of wild Mongols, but I venture to guess this metaphorical example of the mind's inner workings sounds familiar to you. As a saying states: "I have met the enemy and it is I!"

These marauding invaders favorite armaments are fear and negativity. The dirty little trick of the False Self is to divert our attention to our weaknesses rather than focusing on our strengths. Spend time and effort wallowing in the swamplands of weakness and you only sink further, a victim of circumstances rather than rising up to challenge those conditions. These conquered lands go by the names of low self-esteem, depression, and apathy. It is the False Self at work and it will reign as it takes more under its control.

The False Self, ingenious in its survival, can build one's ego with a false sense of confidence that "it's all good!" As we learn more about the False Self, we understand what it's not to do in our lives. Its primary role is not to rule our way of life by regulating the human spirit, mandating the personal experience, or overriding the potential to become. Most important it shouldn't be our "*default mind setting,*" the one we reactively turn to for assistance.

Many pioneers, determined in their quest for a better life, found the journey to new lands terrifying. Despite the fears, a few brave souls blazed new trails in the unknown. They sought a new home for themselves—the home of the brave. The same is true on our inner life's journey. A path lies ahead, but within, as we find our way by the light of understanding.

For the concept of self-awareness, one of the most prevalent metaphors is the reference to light for its meaning, and described as "an ongoing attention to one's internal states.[1]" Too much too soon, and we may be "blinded by

---

[1] (Goleman, 1995)

the light." We then close our eyes to insights we're neither ready to see, nor willing to acknowledge, and above all, afraid to face. We deny the light.

This is the challenge as stated by Plato who said: "*We can easily forgive a child afraid of the dark, the real tragedy of life is when men are afraid of the light.*"[2] Plato's message, and that of many other wise teachers since, is simple: *See the light to wake up and live!*

Awaken and Come Alive! presents the light through the power of self-awareness and provides **Five Master Keys** for life success found within:

1. **Invisible Forces**
2. **Order**
3. **Creativity**
4. **Change**
5. **Relationship**

These are the keys you never lose, but often need to be recovered. While these keys can be identified separately, they are intimately engaged in oneness but not sameness. Influential and inseparable in their actions, they are natural teamworkers. They are perfect collaborators, always

---

[2] (Plato: Brainy Quotes, 2021)

present, working in the Now, often as "silent partners," but "speak loudly" in the self-work produced. Although we have little problem with being continuously engaged in life's activities, troubles occur when we lose our conscious awareness with who's doing the doing. Hence from our master mind keys emerge "key whole" questions regarding our access for self-improvement:

- How can I manage the *unseen* that affects my life?
- How can I promote *order* in my life?
- How can I *create* possibilities for the life I desire?
- How can I be *change* ready for what comes my way?
- How can I cultivate positive and productive *relationships*?

We can begin to unlock answers with our first Master Key of Invisible Forces for entering the inner house to see the unseen.

SECTION I.
Master Invisible Forces

Managing the unseen

When I was a small child, I believed the trees created the wind because I noticed when the trees bowed and the leaves trembled, there was wind. I did not understand that invisible forces were at work so *the effects I saw, I believed were the causes.* This example of a child's misinterpretation of reality provides a critical insight: *Our invisible forces within are the unseen motivators that influence our human behavior.*

Every action originates from an invisible force, an energy that not only moves our minds but moves our bodies. There's more to life than meets the eye, or the "see it to believe it" worldview. Interestingly, a child's misinterpretation can be an adult misunderstanding since the mind more readily grasps what is concrete than abstract, as we rely heavily on our five senses. We may be wide awake, but unaware, because the unseen and untouchable are hidden in the forms we are not accustomed to perceiving.

Although we can't see them with the naked eye, we know the existence of gravity, energy, and atomic particles. These forces are undeniable laws, but not undefinable that work the same for all of us. Once we become aware of our unseen motivators, our "invis-abilities," we can develop our ability in their proper use for enhancing our lives.

Got Roots?

Here's an exercise that illustrates the common oversight of invisible forces in our lives. Take a moment and draw, or visualize, a tree.

Got it? What does your tree look like? If you are like most people, you didn't include in your drawing or visualization, the roots of the tree. Of course, we know the roots are very much a part of the tree and in fact the most important element from which the tree derives its very life. Yet, roots are easy to overlook. We may forget to include them because we don't see below the surface. Just because we don't see it, doesn't mean it doesn't exist. Hence, out of sight can be out of mind, and so it is that we most often draw a tree without its roots.

When it comes to our own lives we barely scratch the surface. We must dig deeper to see the fact of life: *The fruits of your labor are the result of the roots of your behavior.*

This unseen world is the essential part of all of nature. These invisible forces are powerful, especially when observed as acts of nature. For example, one day Utah's famous natural rock formation located in the Arches National Park, the Wall Arch, "decided to let go" and collapsed as it yielded to natural forces. The Parks Chief wisely commented, "They all let go after a while."[3]

Here's another example of the power of natural invisible forces. On a particularly windy day, a tall pine tree outside my office blew over. The mighty invisible force of the wind toppled this magnificent tree that stood firmly there for many years. Sorry to see, but a fact of life.

As created by natural forces, the Wall Arch and the tree's eventual downfall were from natural forces. They stood the test of *some* time. Even being "solid as a rock" or firmly grounded is temporary and sustained only under certain conditions.

Structures fall by natural forces and in turn create new ones. The rock formation or the tree had no choice in the matter but to yield to the influences that bear upon them. The human, however, has choices. We can create the conditions that are favorable to our existence in the way that we desire to live. In fact, these invisible forces can

---

[3] (Stark, 2008)

be utilized for our own growth and development that will make us stronger.

So, how will you build your life structure to withstand the natural forces that if left unattended may tear you down? Will you be "asleep at the will," or will you awaken and arouse the powers within to come alive? We can re-create and reinforce our lives through the power of our invis-abilities.

Be First, then Do

Most of our formal education and training is about acquiring the knowledge *to do*. It's remarkable the level of expertise in doing one can achieve. Basically, we learn to take mastery over the outside world, the environment within which we operate. However, when we find ourselves in the other kind of deep "doo, doo" (internal trouble and conflict), it is our *being* that must come to the aid of our inner world. This *light in shining armor* is our True Self.

Many successful and happy people know how to do one thing very well: *they know how to live from the inside out*. They are untouchable from the outside but in touch with themselves on the inside. They are master craftsmen and women who practice the cultivation of the life bearing secret seeds: *they value continuous learning, they know how to do effectively, and they know themselves well*. In doing so, they take self-control. As a result, they know who and what they are, and perhaps more importantly, they know what they are not. They soar with their strengths. They *rest assured* with the ability to *withstand* the winds of adversity as they stand strong because of *understanding*. They sow the secret seeds to reap success by being grounded on the underlying principle of inner-self work: *We are humans "being" first, humans "doing" second.*

This art of self-leadership is defined as: *The ability to be consciously aware of the powers within to direct the inner resources of the self for positive and productive results.*

Regardless the level of education, or the mastery of skills for doing, it does not necessarily mean one has learned about oneself to have gained *self-mastery*. Nor is it assured we are wiser in our older age, or happier through what we've achieved or acquired. I know people with a B.A., Ph.D., J.D., M.D., C.E.O. and just about every other combination of letters, but I have yet to meet anyone with G.O.D. after their name! The point is, there is always more to know about what's going on *"in here"* and no one has all the answers for what's going on *"out there"* but there's something *"up above"* that can help. So, what's up?

What's up is a higher educational endeavor at a deeper level for understanding the Self. It is a learning experience like none other. This exploration of the nature of our being for going above and beyond the traditional schools of thought for learning and our usual practice of doing is *Self-study.*

There is more to be, in order to do, and there is more to do in order to be. It's about learning what's going on in *you* through *insight* that instructs the toughest lessons in life, often acquired through the school of hard knocks, yet the most rewarding. Truly a study in itself by the Self, and thank G.O.D. for this ability! Self-awareness provides us with the ability to declare: *"I see the I."*

In this section we will examine our most powerful invis-abilities to shine the light through our **Attention, Attitude, Beliefs, Will, and Emotions** for enhancing our lives. These essential life forming elements underlie the principle of the first Master Key of Invisible Forces to help us awaken and come alive by understanding that:

Forces shape form—all originates from invisible forces.

CHAPTER ONE
You're It!

Seek the Hidden!

I remember as a kid one of the first times I learned how to manage the unseen was through the game of hide and seek. A group of us would gather in the alley. The first order of business was to determine who was going to be "it." We would form our circle with both hands clenched and held in front to begin. "One potato, two potato, three potato, four…" Around we would go till the last one counted out was designated as "it." The "it" would cover his/her eyes and count to twenty while the rest went to hide.

Few of us ever wanted to be "it." It was you against them. It meant being alone on your quest. There was a feeling of separation from the others. You may have felt different being "the odd one out." There was the sensation of *unseen forces* working against you in achieving your intentions. In other words, your goal of finding your hidden friends was in conflict with their collective goal of not being found. Most important, we played the game. We were after all, duty bound by the role of being "it," the seeker.

The Haunt in the Hunt

There was an old abandoned house near the alley where we played. For some of us, the ram-shackled house was considered haunted. It was a scary place to enter, because we believed there were some invisible forces in there like ghosts, as well as live creatures such as rats and spiders. The old and flimsy floorboards were a threat to give way, causing one to literally fall through the cracks!

Our parents warned us it was off limits and to stay out. Often there were one or two kids, usually older and a bit wiser, who had no fear of entering the house. They used this to their advantage to stay hidden. A defining moment in the game, especially for the "it," came about when all were found except one or two, perhaps hidden in the scary house. As the evening darkness set in, some of us dared not go in. This was the turning point and often the game then ended. The search was over, along with the possibility of "winning." Something unfounded and unseen had won us over. The fear and the darkness had beaten us.

The Window of Opportunity

The choice to see what's inside the inner house of the self can be scary. As in the game of Hide and Seek, it's a mind game. After all, it's where our own demons reside, the images that haunt, and what we don't want to face about ourselves that can stop us in our tracks. This hesitancy denies us a most critical opportunity. This is the entrance exam to the most important institution for higher learning of self-knowledge. The price of admission is the admission of these fears.

Now imagine yourself in a dark house and there is a window where light has found its way through. Looking closely at the beam of light that slices through the darkness, you notice the particles of dust that swirl within. You realize then, by the light that exposes them, that the dark space was not empty. These can serve as a metaphor for our thoughts and the power of association.

Entering our mind are free-flowing thoughts. As we grasp onto a thought with attention, the law of attraction is set in motion pulling in similar thoughts demonstrating that "like attracts like" as a critical mass of "like mindedness" forms. We begin to "connect the thoughts." When you are aware of this interior free-flowing thought stream, you have gained an important insight of seeing your thoughts separate from the observer, then a higher self sees above all else, and allows access to an important self-awareness tool.

Do AWAY with IT!

One of the advantages we have is the ability to *think about what we think about.* We can learn to develop this ability by choosing not to hold onto a troublesome thought, and instead *Do AWAY with IT* with the following AWAY acronym that will help settle some of the mind's dust particles:

1. **A—Acknowledge IT:** Recognize its presence. Be conscious of the thoughts that are producing anxiety, worry, fear, or other negative emotions.

2. **W—Witness IT:** Be present and centered with the self. Be watchful of what's going on in the inside of you.

3. **A—Allow IT:** Don't resist the thought or deny your feelings. Allow it to proceed on its way out. Remember thoughts move, so keep them on the move.

4. **Y—You're IT!:** Remember you're "it!" Take responsibility for managing your own Intrusive Thoughts (IT).

This AWAY with IT is an awareness exercise that takes practice to bring to light the thought process and recalls the power in "letting go" of thoughts. It is an exercise in consistency of practice for the mastery of mindset, not for perfection. You then can Acknowledge, Witness, Allow, and engage Your response in managing the Intrusive Thoughts (IT).

I remember the day I mustered up the courage to enter the scary house in the alley. To my relief, I discovered none of the dreaded terrors, like ghosts, were real! It was as if seeing on my own, caused the terrors to magically disappear. I applied the test of truth and the practical experience changed my preconceived notions. Yes, it was important to be aware of real dangers that may be on the inside, like a rusty nail ready to stick me in the foot! However, when the fear is managed through a more secure self, you can then focus your attention on what's real.

The great self-development master, Vernon Howard declared: "it is healthy to yearn for the way out of your haunted house."[4] The signs of self-awareness point the way, the way of contrary where our exit is the entrance, the regress is the progress, and to get out we must go in. If there is something drawing you inward to seek the hidden way out, answer the call. This calling can be a simple attention-getter like a light tapping on your shoulder and politely asking: "Excuse me. May I have your attention for a moment?"

---

4   (Howard, 1967)

There is a higher Self that stands behind and desires to provide us with *the right direction which is the light direction*—a way out. These *light* taps can be ignored but will come to us over and over as an invitation to change. They are "for warning" signals to *awaken*. Left unattended or ignored, they can become a *"slap,"* a command to change, such as a crisis where you have little choice but to face the presenting challenge to your well-being. These "slaps" are much more forceful than the "taps" and ask: "Now do I have your attention?" It can be a rude awakening!

How will you answer the call? Will it be a return to the beaten path (the same response) that has beaten you up (the same result) time and time again (the same repeating pattern) only to find yourself: *here again* (the same place)? Instead of the same thing, there can be "something entirely different." Just as surely as the light shining through the window exposing the dust particles, when you *consciously pay attention*, you shine the light of awareness on your own thought particles.

CHAPTER TWO
Focus your Attention

Stay Awake!

Have you ever been in a conversation when suddenly you realize you hadn't heard a word of what's been said? Have you ever driven down the street, when suddenly you get the strange sensation of coming awake from being "asleep at the wheel?" Did I just stop at a green light and drive through a red one? When we awaken and come alive to the present moment, we may wonder: where was I? We may not even remember getting aboard that runaway train of thought!

We've all experienced times when we don't attend to the moment. That's why it's referred to as *being* present not *doing* present. You have to *be here in the now*.

What is it that draws your attention? The answer to this is: "attractors." An attractor, as defined for our self-work, is simply: *something that draws your attention.* Attractors are powerful because anything that attracts your attention requires an investment of energy, as well as other resources including time and money. Hence attention is an investment, and we should be concerned for our return on the investment. Dr. David R. Hawkins, author and spiritual teacher, provides a critical insight in his book, Power vs. Force, regarding the power of attractors. Dr. Hawkins states that all the great teachers throughout time have simply taught the importance to: *give up weak attractors for strong attractors."* [5]

Give it Up to Live it Up!

It is a critical insight for the individual who desires a more meaningful, purposeful experience to understand the substance of one's authentic life. We can begin by taking a personal inventory of our attractors in life. We must discern the artificial from the real, the essential ingredients from the additives. We then realize what is no longer fruitful for our natural growth to allow renewal to take place.

When we arrive at this turning point in our lives of choosing a new direction, we come to a time that requires personal assessment. It means you take a personal inventory of all aspects of your life to assess your health, career and work, financial fitness, relationships, and your spirituality. Can you identify the attractors that drain your energy and overly consume your inner resources?

---

[5] (Hawkins, 2002)

What about those things or activities that energize and strengthen your life.

As life unfolds, one senses that there is more ahead and something greater that lies above at a higher level. What is ahead of you? For most people it is the fulfillment of expectations, pleasurable desires, plans, and the anticipation of positive outcomes and results. What lies above you? For most, it is a life standard, the goal, the purpose, the Truth, the Light, or any other name you choose to call it. It is the natural sense that there is something worth striving for, something greater than our present self. A new, improved version of life to the next level that in fact requires movement.

Moving forward to a more rewarding and fulfilling life requires giving some of yourself up in order to live closer to your True self. For anything we move toward, we must also move away from something. This is challenging growth because it means giving up some of our most cherished and habitual ways of being and doing. It means examining our patterns of thinking by identifying our routines and our predictable responses, some of which do not serve us well.

Our thoughts are energized and have the power to draw our attention which in turn attracts more of the same. This is the return on your investment for what you've spent your attention on. This "attractive" nature of ours means we can draw to us the thoughts that are life promoting (strong attractors), as well as thoughts that are self-defeating (weak attractors).

A definition for *attend* is to be present, to apply the mind, or pay attention.[6] We have to *stay awake,* which can be our most challenging task. We're not "all here" when we "fall asleep." To awaken and come alive, we must come to our senses.

Sensei of the Senses

In the martial arts the most powerful technique in self-defense is not about "kicking ass" but a little higher in the anatomy—training a disciplined mind, for *being* prepared before *doing*. The martial arts are first and foremost the *mental arts*. As a student of Shotokan karate, I heard one word more than any other from the sensei, our master teacher. While drilling us in our workouts, he repeated one word: "focus, focus, focus!"

We were being trained (and strained) in how to act in self-defense with the solid foundation provided by certain stances like the Kiba Dachi position, one of many that focus on mastering opposites like stability and mobility. It was one of my first experiences with understanding the

---
6   (Merriam-Webster, 2021)

role of *opposites,* how two things can exist in one position that seem contradictory. This awareness with practice, gave me a third option in how to effectively apply them for one's benefit.

Whether it be for self-protection or self-correction, we "take a stance" in order to learn how to ACT under certain conditions. Three principles for an "in-stance" include: Awareness, Centered, and Test (ACT). Being in stance means you can respond in an instance! Through the practice of ACT: *We learn to hold our inner-ground (**Awareness**) to be grounded in our stance (**Centered**) to best face the circumstance (**Test**) that threatens our well-being.*

We live with the threat of chaos that will scatter our attention, create disorder, and make us vulnerable to the slightest wind of adversity. When invisible forces work against us, such as a lack of attention, our performance is weakened.

Focused attention is one of the most effective ways of accomplishing a goal with the greatest assurance of a quality outcome as demonstrated in the ability to be single-minded in purpose. This is like a laser that gathers up the diffused light particles and aligns them, focused and ordered, creating the power to cut through steel. The light bulb, on the other hand, scatters its light particles and uses more energy, displaying chaotic behavior. Its "attention" is everywhere. As a result light bulbs eventually burn out. When we are focused and ordered, coherence emerges. We become powerful in the efficient use of our energy in effectively cutting through the chaos.

There's a popular concept that robs us of our focused attention. It is referred to as multi-tasking. It's probably responsible for more accidents, shoddy work, and burnout than any other single factor. We may attempt to do several things at once, but can only give one thing our undivided attention. Our minds cannot *multi-think*. Our thoughts, come in one at a time, vying for our attention. Avoid being a victim of circumstances, be a sensei of the senses. ACT and remain stable yet mobile, and remember to: focus, focus, focus!

Practice the following strategies to reinforce focused attention:

1. **Practice the Do AWAY with IT exercise:** Manage your thoughts.

2. **Communicate Attention:** Show interest, provide feedback, and listen.

3. **Exercise the mind and body:** Practice meditation and other activities to manage your time and stress. Schedule a daily timeout from technology.

4. **Go to the SPA:** Attend to your physical living space. Our environment provides many distractions. Focus and develop your attention by maintaining a Safe, Peaceful, and Attractive (SPA) home.

5. **PAIN:** Remember PAIN as an acronym that stands for *Paying Attention Is Needed*. Physical and emotional pain are signs of disorder. Give it due attention before it gets worse.

CHAPTER THREE
Shape your Attitude

Create a "to be" list

In my training workshops, I often use an icebreaker I call "Life is a Bowl of Cherries." I hand out a paper with a picture of a bowl filled with red cherries. I explain that the cherries represent what they hold as "good" in their lives. I ask the participants to write down the things they enjoy doing, such as their interests, passions, hobbies, and the people that are important to them. In fact, while they are completing the assignment, I will jot down the top three answers that I believe will emerge. Generally, the most common answers are: time spent with family, enjoying the outdoors, and travel. We then share our "cherries" in life, and we come to know each other a little better.

This exercise is insightful particularly regarding human motivation, as it reveals what individuals identify with and what they spend their attention, energy, time, and money on. Their "cherries" are what *moves* them to do. They define what adds meaning and happiness to their lives and represent powerful personal "drivers" as they seek to fulfill those desires. It also shows how much we have in common in the things we often pursue and enjoy.

Cherries or Pits?

So, what's in your bowl? Is it half empty or half fulfilled? An improved mind shift in positive thinking is when one declares "life is a bowl of cherries" versus "life is the pits!" We desire to avoid the opposite of our "cherries," so we *cherish the cherries and spit the pits!* However, it is through self-awareness that we realize that the "pits" too have a "moving effect" on us. When we take time to examine the "cherries" in our lives, we take stock in the "good" we have in our lives. This reminds us of what we need to do to maintain our cherished cherries, and more importantly how we need *to be*.

To be or not to be, that is the Answer!

What kind of experience do you want to have? Will you choose joy or sorrow, a positive outlook or a negative view? Will you try something new or will you hesitate to proceed into the dark woods?

Many of us regularly write a daily "to do" list, and may never have considered a "to be" list. As a result, we may overlook a critical life success principle: *The quality of an experience and the outcomes of our performance have everything to do with our being, the state of our mind.*

Our "To Be" list is positive mental preparation for the real experience. This is the content of the nature of our thoughts to set the mind stage for the performing act. It creates the context of the quality of the experience and along the way, the results of our doing.

Your becoming has everything to do with the outcome that is the result of your incoming thoughts. How might you prosper if only you make a choice *to be* a certain way before you set out *to do?* For example, ask yourself before you begin and after all is said, but not yet done:

- What kind of day do I desire to have? After all, it's mine to live.

- Beyond all I have to do (quantity), what kind of being (quality) do I hope for by the end of the day? After all, I have to live with myself.

- What do I intend to gain from an experience? After all, every experience is a learning opportunity.

- How might I prepare emotionally for what I am to do? After all, performance is fueled through emotions.

- What kind of mindset prior to any event or interaction will promote the possibility of a positive and productive experience? After all, results do matter.

How often do we set ourselves up for failure before getting out of the starting gates? The outcomes may be the result of a substandard performance when we are unaware that *the thought process produces the product.* Believe it or not, a failure or a bad experience is predictable. Success is first and foremost a state of being rather than doing.

Our "To Be" list has the power to create the conditions we meet. This success secret is revealed when we consider to: *Think that way,* **to be** *that way, before* **you do**. Be the way you want to do and you will be there before you do. This means you begin with the end in mind. Your attitude will drive the nature of your course.

Preparing for the Real Experience

I work with military veterans providing educational and transitional services for success in college. Some of our veteran students have combat experience. I am always amazed that the biggest fear for some of these field-tested fighters, who know the ravages of war, is the fear of stepping into a classroom. For some, just the prospect of setting foot on a college campus is scary.

This is one example of a greater issue many veterans face in the challenge of making the transition from military to civilian life, particularly for those who have experienced combat. These are warriors who fight another foe: *An intimate enemy.*

In his book, *Managing Transitions,* William Bridges states that it isn't the changes that do you in, it's the transitions.[7] Life changes, but how we get through life is what matters. How we deal with the real, the truth through the test of time, is what's relevant. In fact, with any goal we set our sights on, we are driven by our current reality, a reality that we want to change, to a new reality we want to experience.

Some combat veterans in transition are further debilitated from post-traumatic stress disorder (PTSD). The effect of PTSD is an example of how one's experience can dramatically affect one's reality and how that impacts all other experiences. Most veterans, like others who have experienced a traumatic event, prefer not revisiting the past experience. They have walked the talk, but most prefer not talking about the walk. Nonetheless, these people are survivors. They are warriors who now must become peaceful warriors to survive.

Veterans are keenly aware that they share an uncommon experience and as a result have a unique and

---

[7] (Bridges, 1993)

strong camaraderie with those who've *really* "been there." However, one of the hallmarks of the program's success is to treat each veteran as an individual and acknowledge his or her personal experience as their own. Although it's easy to generalize and categorize, everyone's experience is different. Rather than trying to fit them into a mold, we help shape new perceptions (I see) for their own success (I can do).

One of the principles we base our helping services for success in higher education, is the same philosophy underlying the purpose of these veterans' previous military training: *The need to be prepared for what they will have to do.*

We provide the "near experience" of the real thing with the goal of achieving a college degree. We want them to *awaken and come alive*! We want them to be the Self that can succeed. We care, we don't scare them straight. We bring to light their fears and needs, providing resources and learning opportunities that will lead to new ways. They are being prepared, trained on *how to be before they go and do*.

The time comes when the veteran student has stayed the course of new learning and is prepared for enrollment into college, the real thing. As in any new experience we must apply ourselves otherwise it is hearsay, *a near experience*. It's the next step up. However, in *doing so* we should be aware of the importance of *being so*. This means that the nature of our being determines the nature of our doing. What's on your "to be" list?

The Be Attitudes

A "to be" list should include one critical check off: *Check your attitude.* For example, take a look at the following attitudes in need of adjustment:

- If you've made up your mind on having a negative experience, you're going to find yourself stuck in a lot of "yuck."

- If you are impatient you will find yourself with a lot of "wait" on your shoulders.

- If you are in a rush, all the rest of us will seem to be at rest and in your way.

- If you plan on engaging in conflict, you've already beaten yourself up.

- If you're going in to raise a big stink, chances are you won't come out smelling like a rose.

- If the underlying motive is to find fault with someone, that's what you will find—a great divide between you and that person.

- If your desire is to stir things up, you're going to be the swizzle stick and life is on the rocks!

The bottom line that should be top of mind is the following: *"Being" has everything to do with intention.* A positive attitude can promote a positive experience. It is a true principle: *what you project is what you attract.* The concept of "to be" means: *To be conscious of the power of our thoughts to affect the outcomes of our doing.*

To achieve mastery in self-awareness, as in all arts, we must practice. To be an accomplished *thought-leader* means *we take responsibility for the way we think and therefore the way we follow.* We can more easily carry out our practical duties, feel happiness, exude a confidence, and experience a productive day with energy to spare when we "make up our mind" *to be* a certain way. When we remain cognizant of this concept, we then realize *there are no bad days but instead only bad ways.* We then understand it makes more sense to ask: *"Hey, how you being? Have a nice way!"*

The state of being is a *process not a product.* Our greatest experiences are based on the power of *being not doing.* We see this power manifest itself in some of my favorites as in: *being present, being peaceful, being happy, being healthy, being a friend, being compassionate,* and the greatest power on earth: *being in love.*

Greater benefits can be had through the process of being. When we learn more about the "being" of ourselves we understand better the actions and behavior of our "doing." Here is the valuable insight: *As we understand ourselves better, we can better understand others. As we create an improved self-relationship, we automatically create improved relationships with others.* Therefore: *The quality of the "inner-action" determines the quality of the interaction.* It is through an attitude that we plant the seeds of well-being for life to be fruitful not pitiful.

Viktor Frankl, an Austrian psychiatrist, and Holocaust survivor stated that "the last of the human freedoms is to choose one's attitude in any given circumstances."[8] Mr. Frankl knew something about the power of attitude and its role in strengthening the will to survive and to thrive.

---

8 (Frankl, 2006)

CHAPTER FOUR
Strengthen the Will

Get back on your life cycle

I was down at the schoolyard that day when I decided to give it a try. My big brother helped me onto the seat, steadied me, and then gave the bike a push! I was on my way and on my own. Oh no! At first, what fear, and then, what a thrill!

Do you recall when you learned how to ride a bicycle? Perhaps it seemed impossible to do. You had seen others do it and the fun they were having, but you hadn't ever tried it. Then one day the moment of truth arrived just for you. It came first as an "overriding" urge, when your desire to ride a bike was stronger than your fear it couldn't be done. The time was right. You were ready. You awkwardly climbed aboard the bicycle seat. Perhaps a parent, or an older sibling was there as a steady hand to give you a push. Then the rest was up to you! You realized you couldn't stand still to proceed, and you certainly couldn't look back as you knew that wouldn't help! Your gaze was fixated straight ahead as you steered crookedly down the path. As you gripped the handle bars tighter, fear gripped you in a last ditch effort to keep you from moving ahead that may very well have put you in the ditch! Your determination increased as you kept pedaling, and amazingly the ride became smoother, balanced, and easier. Fear left you as the adrenaline rush of excitement and joy took its place. You had done it! There was a feeling of exhilaration, a sense of freedom under your own power to create the very momentum to propel yourself down the road. You had done the impossible! You had overcome your fears. You had taken mastery over the bicycle and you would never forget how to ride a bike. It marked a turning point going forward, and there would be no turning back. It was an example of true empowerment when your personal effort was rewarded, and it all began with your willingness to try.

The Magic Word that Turns the Will

Try is the magic word that turns the will. It's good to try new things. Otherwise one would have never climbed onto that bike. Where does the desire to "try" come from? Trying is effort, an energy that comes from within. Underlying every trial of effort, is the power of the will. Common descriptors of the will include persistence, commitment, motivation, and yes, a bit of stubbornness. As we pedal our way of the will in life, we should keep in mind the nature of our progression: *Your* *destination (**desire**) has a lot to do with your determination (**will**). Where you arrive (**achieve**) has a lot to do with your drive (**motivation**).*

Buckles and Chuckles

The will to live is powerful and people often demonstrate the phenomenal capacity to beat the odds to "keep on keeping on." Take for example Mr. Frank Buckles. He was America's last surviving World War I veteran who in 2011 lived to be 110 years old. He was the last "doughboy" of over 4,700,000 Americans who served during the Great War. As a civilian, he was even captured as a prisoner of war during World War II and spent more than three years in a Japanese prison camp. Mr. Buckles said while genetics, healthy eating, and exercise are vital for a long life, it is *the will to survive* that's most important.[9]

Then there's Claude Stanley Choules—the man known as "Chuckles" to his comrades in the Australian Navy. He was the last combat veteran of World War I. He too died in the same year and the same age as Mr. Buckles! He was a centenarian who swam in the sea, danced, and wrote his first book at the age of 108! He served for 41-years in the military, but Chuckles was happiest being known as a

---

[9] (Patterson, 2011)

dedicated family man. He was married for 76 years.[10] Talk about a survivor!

The interesting parallel lives of Chuckles and Mr. Buckles demonstrated that survivors know how to exercise willpower! These are people who believe life is to be lived. It is a mindset that life is to be cherished not perished. There is a tremendous life force in applying the power of will when we recall our ability to consciously push the undesirable thoughts that deprive rather than thrive out of the way.

Where there's a will, there's a way is perhaps an overused cliché, but underutilized as a skill. As a skill, we can develop it, as suggested by many wise sages throughout history, by becoming aware of its possibility and decide to cultivate it.[11] This is the re-conditioning of our will for what we desire to become.

An important realization in empowering ourselves is to re-capture and develop our will through the power of choice. You have the power to choose how you feel. Why not choose to feel better? We can feel better through our ability to take responsibility for our emotions.

---

10 (New York Times, 2011)
11 (Murphy, 2002)

CHAPTER FIVE
Manage Your Emotions

Put some PEP in your step

You have the power by choice to create an internal mood that will present an external expression. Being gloomy over the gloom does not change the scenery. A dark mood does nothing to clear the mind's sky of the dark clouds of despair. We remain in the dark when we resist change, avoid contact, deny realities, or we resign ourselves to the belief: "It's just the way it is." Another possibility is that we spread our anger and misdirect our negative responses upon others. Then, what originated as one problem has turned into some other issue taking on a life of its own. The precipitating event may no longer be an issue, as our *solution to the problem becomes the problem.*

In the physical world, motion is energy. In the mind's world, emotions are energized and force does not provide an effective solution. The answer lies in allowing these negatively charged emotional energies their proper course.

Negative feelings can drain you, but your positive feelings can be your productive fuel. We can train our brain for a better performance through better emotional re-conditioning of the will to do, and therefore achieve better results. We can learn to process our emotions in a positive way, rather than being possessed by our emotions in a negative way. This is how we generate *PEP,* your Personal Emotional Power for producing energy and high spirits.

Remember the power of our emotions as an invis-ability: We choose *to affect our inner self and therefore our effect upon the outer world through our emotions.* Practice the following strategies for letting your emotions be, rather than allowing yourself to be your emotions.

Generating P.E.P: Personal Emotional Power

1. **Don't be deceived by what you perceive.**

    What you perceive is never the entire picture of reality. Question the definitive by being inquisitive. Ask questions for clarification.

2. **Learn new problem solving.**

    A negative reaction to a negative comment will not equal a positive outcome.

3. **The upset is a set up.**

   When we get upset we set ourselves up for conflict and poor results. Anger is a negative emotion and left unattended, yields negative results.

4. **Self-assess what can make you a mess.**

   Choose a different response for different results.

5. **Be powerful not forceful.**

   Forge your own way, but don't force your way upon another.

6. **Is it a fact or a feeling?**

   Understand the appropriate and objective use of facts and the subjective expression of feelings.

7. **What in the word is going on?**

   Words are powerful and some carry more emotional weight than others. What you say can make a "word" of difference.

8. **The gift is your presence.**

   Stay centered with the Self and remain in the Now.

9. **Enhance communication.**

   Consider the context within which something is said rather than just the content of what you're hearing.

10. **Permission denied.**

    Don't permit feelings of others to be your own or be told how you are supposed to feel.

11. **Maintain personal boundaries.**

    Cultivating healthy relationships requires setting personal boundaries.

12. **Stop keeping score.**

    Give up keeping score of what someone is or isn't doing. No one has to lose.

13. **Take "response-ability."**

    Manage your thought process and be *apart from* rather than *a part of* negative emotions.

Diffusing the Emotional Mind Field

The practice of developing your emotional control includes some of the following benefits.[12]

---
[12] (Goleman, 1995)

- Managing your feelings for fueling your best performance for productive outcomes.

- Recognizing emotions in others and thereby choosing appropriate and effective responses for sustaining positive and productive relationships.

- Increasing self-awareness by focusing inwardly as you become attentive to the emotionally charged thoughts and feelings.

- Maintaining an inner-peace that is undisturbed by the thoughts or feelings regarding any event, situation, person, or thing.

- Enhancing your well-being by reducing the runaway emotions that rob you of vital energy and drain your inner resources.

- Being happier.

A positive nature can override the negative and creates a feedback loop returning positive energy. You will detect the approaching disturbance and its effect will be lessened. You will minimize the loss of personal energy and the drain on your inner resources that emotional imbalance consumes. By taking "response-ability," you are mindful that you are the creator of your own storms and with practice become a proactive influence upon the number, as well as the duration, of the storms passing through you. Move forward as you diffuse the emotional "mind field" and instead ignite the performance fuel to put some PEP in your step. You WILL it and you will do it!

CHAPTER SIX
Change your Beliefs

The road ahead is in your head

A common saying with a revision states: "nothing ventured in the unknown, nothing gained beyond what we know." Discomfort with uncertainty results from fear of the unknown which keeps us in our place and hinders our forward progress. *Our being afraid is a being that is afraid to do* and it takes us nowhere fast. We become comfortable with what we consider to be the certainty of continuity and we get "blind-sighted" by an "invading" force that takes us over.

I have a friend who is a former Navy SEAL. One day, I asked him if he was ever afraid when performing a dangerous mission. He grew silent and simply raised his arm with his hand held out. It was steady and still. Then he asked me:

"Do you know what that is?

Not knowing where he was going with this, fearful that I'd asked the wrong question, I stepped back a bit.

"No." I answered.

"It's fear under control," he said.

Yes, he knew about fear and yes, fear was there, but he learned how to take control of his fears. His example of a steady hand in the face of fear provides a good insight for self-control: *Your mind is in your hands.*

The road ahead is in your head. This inner drive with a "steady hand" is our desire to maintain *self-control*. Along the way are two common roadblocks that want to interfere with your progress. They are two deceptive cohorts that stand in your way. If we don't learn to control them, we will have our hands full with what's on our mind.

"Inner-fearance"

What is it that unnerves the steady hand? What "orange cones" along your path direct your drive in life? What keeps you from being self-directed? What keeps you from moving ahead is probably not a lack of resources, but a lack of certainty. It is the uncertainty of outcomes that makes most of us uncomfortable. Hence, we resist change or the disturbing event that enters our lives.

We have a hard time tolerating uncertainty that brings with it the fear of the unknown. With fear comes its favorite bosom buddy: *resistance*. Yes, it's a tag team we must face! Time out! Go to your corner but don't throw in the towel, instead awaken and come alive by learning more about this mind-wrestling duo.

Fear and resistance are allies. These mental cohorts are stuck in the rut, holed up in the bunker, as they battle against change and uncertainty by lobbing deceptive and false charges to keep you in your place and better yet, to take you further down. Working closely, they combine forces to become more powerful as they form: *inner-fearance*. The word sounds like interference and that's exactly what it produces when we understand that: *Fear and resistance interfere with our lives and it comes from within.*

Inner-fearance is a control mechanism utilized by the False Self. Rather than holding our hand steady, it gets a grip on us. This means that: *Every time we resist something, it is out of fear; and every time we fear something, we are resisting.*

For example, when things go well, there can be a false sense of security in the belief of permanency in what one has. Hence, we resist change for fear of losing what we have. When things fall apart, we may embrace a false sense of hopelessness with the fear that nothing can be done. We may then resist assistance because we believe it won't make any difference. We may come to embrace the notion that nothing can be done, but nothing can be further from the truth! These are false views of *certainty* rooted in two opposing beliefs to our potential for self-development:

1. I have all the answers to what I face—A false certainty of security.

2. There are no answers to what I face—A false certainty of hopelessness.

We become "know it all's," but ironically with all we know, it doesn't seem to help! For all we know, you never know. Good to know, because never knowing may just save your life, as illustrated in the following true story.

Don't take "Know" for an Answer!

The year is 1967, an 18-year-old high school graduate decides to join the Marines. Across the country is another young man who has joined the Marines too. Soon they will cross paths in a far off land. Both would meet under unbelievable circumstances and both would be fighting for *one* of their lives. A "tag team" of another sort is about to wage a very personal warfare for the welfare of one young warrior. This remarkable true story unfolded during the Vietnam Tet Offensive in 1968, and years later, about a very special reunion as described in the following newspaper article.

U.S. Marine, Gilbert Hernandez was on a tank that was ambushed by the enemy and hit with charges and grenades. Doctors in triage took a look and sent him to the morgue.

Charles Roth was there that day assigned to fingerprint and bag bodies brought to the Graves Registration at Dong Ha, a site closest to the DMZ.

Roth remembers working side-by-side with another Marine fingerprinting and bagging the dead. Then Roth saw something.

"The only reason I noticed Hernandez is because he was the only one moving," Roth said. Sometimes, a body does move in the morgue, from rigor mortis, but something in his stomach moved. I said, 'dude, I think he moved.' Then I saw him twitch again.

Roth took Hernandez back to triage and informed doctors of their suspicions saying, "This guy's still alive."

Roth returned to working on bodies, and Hernandez was brought back out and dropped in the same place.

"They said, 'he's dead now,'" Roth said.

"I looked at him and had a bad feeling. That's when I hit his chest three times. I hit him hard and blood came out of all the bullet wounds, and again he went back to triage.

> *"I'm saying, 'This guy's moving.' We were (ticked). Things were pretty hectic. We were overloaded with bodies and they were overloaded with wounded. It was busy that day. I heard later he was still living, but only knew his name was Hernandez. I had no idea where he was from."*
>
> *"I was told I would never walk, and you can see I'm walking," Hernandez said. "I wanted to die. I told the doctor it hurts too much, and he said, 'it hurts until you get better.'"*
>
> *In the traumatic time Roth spent there, no one left Graves Registration alive — except for Hernandez. "He was the only one that got away. It's not the end, it's the beginning," Roth said.*
>
> *Hernandez says his name would be on the Vietnam Wall were it not for Roth, his own mother's prayers and God.*[13]

"Graves" (Charles Roth's nickname), would not take "know" for an answer. This real-life story is an example that we should never give up (hopelessness), nor should we ever believe we know it all (certainty). Nor should we readily believe or accept, what someone else says is the truth. What we think we know can be far from the truth.

---

13   (Reilly, 2011)

Despite doctors giving up on Lance Corporal Hernandez and pronouncing him dead three times, Roth refused to believe it, and he took action to summon the doctors to take another look, and another, and yet another. He didn't give up on life. He didn't give my brother up. He didn't take even the "certainty" of death as the truth. He was fighting for the life of my brother who was fighting for his life, and made a critical move of his own. It was a *move,* a twitch, that *awakened* Roth for my brother to *come alive!*

This young Marine was pronounced dead by medics not once, not twice, but three times. Yet today, Gil is alive and well. "Ooh Rah!" as the Marines would say, and "thank you God" as Mom would say!

This US Marine, my brother, summed up the experience to me one day, when he simply said: "You just never know." Semper Fi, brother! Enough said!

The Upper Hand

The two certainties of security and hopelessness represent a very common thinking trap as examples of polarized thinking that can compromise our self- control. We get caught up in the either/or, the right and wrong, the this or that, your side and my side, life or death. Welcome to the inner *world of opposites*. It can become a tangled mindset, a strange loop, where we can falsely believe that we're moving on, only to return to the same place. This same place, the result of the same way of thinking, is a repetition of the same thought pattern. The result: *I am here, again*! The only way out of this tangled mess is to rise above it with a new perspective.

The artist M.C. Escher illustrates this abstract idea of a tangled mind and offers a way out of the trap of inner-fearance.[14] Escher's painting called *Drawing Hands* depicts two hands that are identical, each holding a pencil, and each appears to be drawing the opposite hand. I often use this painting in seminars to help understand the abstract world of the opposites in our mind. I display a slide of the *Drawing Hands* and ask the participants: "Which hand is drawing which hand?" This always opens up what I call a "can of squirms" because it makes people uncomfortable. From the body language, I can see the thinking going on and the tension setting in. People grapple for an answer. Some readily state that it's one of the hands but don't agree on which one. Most have no answer, yet most want to give an answer. After a bit of "squirms" I offer them an answer which is the way out: "Neither hand is drawing the other. The artist's hand drew them!" Then I often get some "oohs and aahs," along with a few good natured "boos and hisses!"

---

14 (Goswami, 1993)

This example provides a strategy for a way out of the tangled mess by rising to a different perspective. It points out a reality that didn't appear until a new perspective was offered. Instantly there is relief from the frustration of what we grapple with and makes us squirm in the world of opposites that offers only two choices. By rising above, we find a way out of the tangled mess and see that both opposites exist. It's not my way or your way, it is the High way when we understand that both can peacefully co-exist. The conflict is resolved and the tension released when we acknowledge them as two parts of the whole, a whole that is greater than all the parts. We then can find our way out of the world of opposites with its challenges of dilemma and limiting choices.

A partial self-life lacks wholesomeness and we can become a tangled mess. We become a conflicted self. Fear and resistance should not dominate the greatness of the whole of your life. The True Self offers you a hand up and a hand out of the conflict of the world of opposites. There is a greater whole of you, the artist at work, a True Nature that is above all else. It helps to get out of something in order to let it go!

Get Out and Let Go

The following Zen story illustrates what I mean by a change of perspective for *getting out* of and *letting go* of some of what we've come to know:

> *Nan-in, a Japanese master, received a university professor who came to inquire about zen. Nan-in served tea. He poured his visitor's cup full, and then kept on pouring.*
>
> *The professor watched the overflow until he no longer could restrain himself. "It is overfull. No more will go in!"*
>
> *"Like this cup," Nan-in said, "you are full of your own opinions and speculations. How can I show you Zen unless you first empty your cup?"*[15]

This story's basic message is: *How can you be shown otherwise if you are so immersed in other ways?*

We can be so full of ourselves. Essentially learning for living is about "emptying the cup" of some of what we know to make room for the new. This is how the *knew* becomes the *new*. What you thought you knew is replaced with something new. To be in the *now* is to get out of the *know* that claims: *I know all the answers or I know nothing can be done.* Instead we should proclaim: *What we can only know is the now and that is all we need to know for now. The new is in the now.*

To be certain means we will do in a certain way (remember how our *being* affects our *doing*) and represents a "full cup" leaving no room for improvement and worse, no room

---
15 (Reninger, 2020)

for hope. To believe one knows it all or there's nothing at all that can help, are two ends of the same stick. These flimsy certainties are strong enough to impede progress, create limits, and stifle the desire to know more. To build your structure on these two "pillars of support" will mean your inner-house will topple at the slightest breeze of invisible forces. Both keep you in your place, and the only potential they have is to take you further down. There is no upward movement only a downward drawing of the two hands caught up in the conflict of each other. How can you grasp new understanding with your hands full? Neither offers us a way out of what traps us. They represent contradictions that bears the question: *how can one be so certain to believe they are helpless and how can one be so helpless with all their certainty?* There is no help and there is no hope in this mindset. Perhaps these beliefs, better known as limiting beliefs, are lies.

The Lie's the Limit

I live near the beautiful Sierra Nevada mountains where numerous streams and lakes provide some great fishing. So, let me tell you a fish story. Not about the big one that got away, but about the big one that wouldn't let go.

There was an experiment by researchers who placed a big fish into a tank with minnows.[16] The big fish did what

---

16 (Blanchard, Hersey, & Johnson, 1988)

came natural to survive and spent the time eating little fish. After a period of time, the researchers then placed a glass divider into the tank separating the big fish from the little fish. The big fish could see the other fish and continued to go after them only to get banged up by hitting the glass wall that separated them. After a while of trying to no avail, and a sore head, the big fish gave up and stopped trying. Then one day the researcher's removed the glass barrier. What do you think the big fish did within the environment that was once again abundant with accessible food? The big fish did nothing. Instead of living it up, he had given up. The sad ending to this story is that soon the big fish died!

Although plenty of fish to eat, the big fish believed they were not available based on prior experience, and nothing could be further from the truth, short of a reality based on a limited belief. Here's the False Self bait you don't want to take because it's a mistake that can lead to the following: *When you stop trying you start dying!*

There are many "downers" in this fish story that apply to the human life as a result of the illusion of limitation:

- Downers are de-motivators as we come to believe "there's nothing in it for me!"

- Downers can extinguish our "aspire fire" to *try*.

- Downers can give us a false representation that "nothing has changed."

- Downers can create a present reality based on past experience and its consequences will affect the future.

- Downers have the power to influence our behavior to act in a "certain way."

- Downers can be our "glass ceiling." Although opportunities and abundance are present, we see them as unavailable, so we don't make a move. The self-fulfilling prophesy becomes our reality and we don't "move up" because we believe we can't.

- Downers cause our spirit to die because we are starved for what feeds our purpose.

Don't take the mistake bait! Hopelessness and helplessness go hand-in-hand (a tangled mindset: *which hand is drawing your attention?*) as they feed off of each other. Let's get back down to earth with the following insight: *The sky isn't the limit, the lie's the limit.*

If you think you're limited, you are! Where in the world did such a notion of helplessness come from? It's not in the world or anything outside of ourselves, but in our minds. A contributing factor to this unproductive mindset is based on our beliefs. We really ought to be feeding our minds with a PIE instead!.

Your Slice of PIE: See, Saw, Say

Consider the three important ingredients of Perception, Impression, and Expression (PIE) and the critical role they have in creating your lifestyle as defined in the following:

P—Perception (I see): Your point of view of life.

I— Impression (I saw): How you define your life.

E—Expression (I say): What life means to you.

Your *perception* of reality can create an *impression* within resulting in an *expression* through your actions and behavior. What we perceive defines what we believe. The belief is the "tail that wags the dog" of our behavior. However, belief is strongly influenced by what we are thinking, what we know, and the surrounding environment at the time.[17] All of which are changeable. As a result, you can have another slice of PIE that better suits your taste! It means we can change our life by changing our beliefs. Go ahead, have another slice of PIE!

---

17 (Pink, 2009)

Section I. Recap

Our inner world has powerful natural forces that shake and shape our lives, but they are not intended to break us down unless we are unprepared and unaware. When it comes to our lives, we should remember the life serving principle, as stated in the following ditty:

While natural forces may shake it, they don't have to break it, as you rise above it, you can take it, as they are the very substance to make it.

We don't have to be the victim of unseen forces. We can use these forces to move in the direction we desire. The challenge is to move beyond our five senses and develop a sense of connection with what we don't see—a relationship with the unseen life of the inner-self.

While we are used to assessing nature's biological world, peering through a microscope for the discovery of life's secrets, we often find it difficult to self-examine our human nature through the lens of understanding. Why? Because we usually "don't like to go there." We hesitate to enter the inner house of the mind, and the dark woods of the Self where all the real action takes place. Our inner space is the final frontier, and it can be terrifying territory!

Our invisible forces are energy driven, taking on form through our actions and behaviors. What we hold in our hand was first held in our minds. It is the passion that fuels a commitment that turns into a loving relationship. It is an idea that results in a successful business venture. It is the dream of a better future that drives an individual to work hard. Invisible forces fuel our desires to either move away from something we want to avoid, or draw us toward something we want to gain. This is how we process our thoughts for a productive life. Hence, the cognitive *process* creates the behavioral *patterns* by which we build the *structure* of our lives.

Our mental movements are influenced by the strong attractions as well as the distractions that pull our attention. We are moved by the "gravity" of emotions and circumstances. For example, one of our greatest sources of friction is when there is disagreement. Not only with other people, but when our attitude is out of sorts with an opposing point of view. Or an event enters our lives that makes us uncomfortable. We then experience friction in our minds in much the same way as the mechanical force that resists relative motion between two bodies in contact. In our mind it's the uncomfortable feeling we have for example, when faced with a dilemma. When we find ourselves on the "horns of a dilemma" we often respond with resistance and the result is we can't make a mental move.

This mental state can in fact affect us physically as well. Our bodies lack energy and we tire more easily for reasons that are directly related to our psychological state of mind. You can burn a lot of energy going nowhere fast! In this case we become not only the proverbial couch potato but the couch potato head! Our living system knows something is out of sorts. We find ourselves stuck in a rut, or worse become depressed and apathetic. We like to go to and fro, do this and then that, go over hill and over dale, revisit the past and think about the future. In other words, we have a hard enough time sitting still, let alone being inwardly still. It gives us the feeling of movement. You see there is a deeply ingrained primal fear that when the movement stops we're then "laid to rest." Hence, movement makes us feel alive.

Through the awareness of life's natural processes, we recognize how they can work for us. Through this higher recognition: *We become respective of, as well as receptive to, the natural forces intended to sustain rather than drain our lives.* These powerful unseen forces are responsive to the degree that we hone the skills and competencies for their positive and productive use in shaping our lives.

Awaken and cultivate the powerful natural invis-abilities as allied forces that formulate your life and shape your individual outlook. When you consciously observe these invisible forces you will sense the unseen parts of yourself that lead to actions and behavior, in other words, the hidden motivators. You then expose the elements within your inner world and in doing so you empower yourself as a conscious participant in creating the life you choose to live. You see the root causes of the effects upon your life. When you see the tree and its roots you stand firm because you know where you're coming from. You are grounded within from *a firm basis for knowing and acting—the Authentic Self.*

Sway these invis-abilities in your favor *to be moved to do something different* by exercising your ability to:

1. Focus your **Attention** to direct your moves (behavior).

2. Shape your **Attitude** to move in a positive way (experience).

3. Strengthen the **Will** to make a move (empowerment).

4. Manage your **Emotions** to power your moves (performance).

5. Change your **Beliefs** for creating new moves (possibilities).

Our Attention, Attitude, Will, Emotions, and Beliefs serve as our most powerful inner human resources. But, here's the key insight about our invisible forces: *Left unattended they can work against us.* We develop true empowerment when we exercise our ability to assume command over these natural forces. Never fear, as we have four more master keys to help us direct and align our invisible forces for positive, productive, and prosperous results. Let's begin by putting things in ***Order!***

Key Points of Light

- Forces shape form—all originates from invisible forces.

- Through the practice of ACT: We learn to hold our inner-ground (**Awareness**) to be grounded in our stance (**Centered**) to best face the circumstance (**Test**) that threatens our well-being.

- The quality of an experience and the outcomes of our performance have everything to do with our being, the state of our mind.

- Try is the magic word that turns the will.

- We choose to affect our inner self and therefore our effect upon the outer world through our emotions.

- Every time we resist something, it is out of fear; and every time we fear something, we are resisting.

- The road ahead is in your head.

- The inner drive of the "steady hand" is our desire to maintain self-control.

- Fear and resistance interfere with our lives and it comes from within.

- Don't take "Know" for an answer!

- How can you be shown otherwise, if you are so immersed in other ways?

- What we can only know is the now, and that is all we need to know for now.

- The new is in the now.

- The sky isn't the limit, the lie's the limit.

- Your Slice of P.I.E. in Life means your *perception* of reality can create an *impression* within resulting in an *expression* through your actions and behavior.

SECTION II.
Master Order

Promoting order

Long ago, the ancient philosopher Pythagoras looked up and declared a profound insight. He envisioned the universe as a harmoniously ordered whole and named it the Cosmos which meant order and beauty. This order was perceived as harmony — a consonance between ourselves and the universe.[18] Pythagoras saw patterns of truth above at the universal level and reflective below at the human level, and their application to life. After all, anything that holds up the universe surely can be put to good use to uphold our lives. Most profound in Pythagoras' view, is that the design already exists. It's there for our taking for our own making. This means we don't have to re-invent the wheel. A perfectly ordered system is in place for our use. We need only to understand how the system works to make our own inner-world "go round."

There is a proper working order to how our lives can proceed and progress for our well-being. The way we lead

---

18 (Ghyka, 1977)

our lives and the direction we assume has much to do with the order we follow. Living forms adhere to a natural order. There are certain practices that demonstrate a sort of "code of conduct" respective of the universal laws that govern and serve life. This code of conduct represents an order to be followed "as above so below."

Order too can be a customary procedure, a command, an authoritative direction.[19] Something "in order" can mean it's functioning properly. When we pay attention, one can become effective and efficient, a more efficacious way of life through the Master Key of Order that states:

Life naturally proceeds in a proper order.

---

19   (Order: Merriam Webster, 2020)

CHAPTER SEVEN
Holding Patterns

Rise above the self to see the self

I recall another fun activity for discovery called Hidden Pictures, a regular feature in a magazine called *Highlights for Children*. Various objects and animals were hidden within a bigger picture and the task was to find them. What was helpful in the search was the key list of items on what to look for. Some were easy to find while others required more focus and study to locate. Hmmm…is that a leaf in the tree, or a bushy-tailed chipmunk?

I didn't know at the time, but I was learning two secret skills applicable for self-discovery: *Seeing the big picture, and recognizing patterns.*

The work of self-study requires rising above yourself to see the bigger picture of your life and to recognize the patterns of your behavior. It's the only way to take a look at what you've been doing and see what you've been missing through the process of seeking and finding order in the chaos.

No wonder we like to look up to the stars; something up there rings true for us down here. Something down here looks like something up there. Redundancy and similarity of patterns are evident at the universal level, in biological forms, and in the organization of our lives. As we rise above, we see below to unfold a mental map showing us the patterns of our mindscape that identifies the details of the road ahead. Patterns give away the order of our ways.

You "R" Your Patterns

One of the secrets for being on our way in a new direction, is to see our "ways" from a higher vantage point. Seeing the "big picture" can mean we have the ability to look from a distance, to rise above, and in doing so recognize the defining features upon our mindscape as a result of having a higher point of view. These defining features are *patterns* and give themselves away by displaying distinguishing and recurring marks like an imprint. They make an *impression*.

One of the reasons we're able to differentiate whether it's a leaf or a bushy-tailed chipmunk in the Hidden Pictures game is because of *pattern recognition.* As we look closely and take note, a familiar pattern reveals itself that all is not what it appears to be and *it is what it is*. Just like the object in *Highlight's* Hidden Pictures, it's there; we just have to seek it and see it for ourselves. Pattern recognition allows us to recognize it for what it is. We now see the difference because we know the difference. Hence, patterns make a difference not only in what we see, but what we do and how we do. As such, pattern recognition is an important life success skill that will help us seek and find *self-control.*

In terms of human behavior, patterns constitute a reliable sample of traits, acts, tendencies, and other observable characteristics of a person for insights into how one thinks and essentially how one lives. We can identify our behavioral patterns, the usual order we follow, through the following **Five Rs for Pattern Recognition:**

R1. ROUTINES: Our usual pattern of **habits**. Our standard set of *activity.*

R2. RESPONSES: Our usual pattern of **reactions**. Our standard ways of *replying.*

R3. REQUIREMENTS: Our usual pattern of **preferences**. Our standard *desires.*

R4. RELATIONSHIPS: Our usual pattern of **connections**. Our standard *engagements.*

Together these four Rs create a fifth R that serves as our *frame of reference* described in the following:

R5. REFERENCE: Our usual pattern of **experiences**. Our standard source of *practice.*

Life Frame

Just like a picture in a frame, we do the same with our lives. *We frame our experience.* Our habits, reactions, preferences, and connections become a reference guide for how we proceed and progress with our lives. They create the *order* we follow. Our reference serves as a handy guide because it represents the experience we always draw upon. Like the artist's brush strokes on the canvas, we paint the picture of our own lives. We tend to qualify ourselves based on our experience and it creates an image of who we are. These Five Rs can become our "comfort food for thought," and feed our comfort zone. These are the elements that create our sense of continuity in life. They become our self-identity.

Our ability to see the bigger picture and recognize patterns by their detailed and defining characteristics, as described in finding the Hidden Picture mentioned earlier, offers another valuable insight for self-discovery: *The answers to what you are looking for in the bigger picture we call life, lie within, but you must consciously seek them out by rising above.* In doing so, an order will emerge from the chaos, as you recognize the patterns of your thinking that create the way of your life. You see yourself, and that is the hallmark of self-awareness.

Pattern recognition is a valuable technique for not only identifying the details of our own life, but recognizing the ways of others. We can utilize the Five Rs to see what we must to highlight areas for self-improvement, as well as for performance management. This new perspective allows us to differentiate the parts of our lives that make up the whole of our life. It provides a method of introspection for quality of self-control as we check our life design for areas of improvement.

We seek to have the parts moving, not necessarily in the same direction because that may be the wrong way, but instead the *right* direction for one self. *Be first* with purpose in mind and *do second* as you know the answers to the greater questions of *Why*, and trust that the *how* will follow.

We have a lot of moving parts in our lives but not one or many can be greater than the whole of our lives. The devil can be in the details when a part of our lives dominates as if it were the whole of our lives creating stress and imbalance, and we lose a bit of the authority over our own life.

The Law of Proper Authority

Pythagoras was wise in his description of the universe as an ordered whole displaying harmony and beauty. One of the challenges of self-growth is to find order out of chaos. Just like the water that seeks the path of least resistance, there are other ways and means (an order) that won't lead to dead ends, but instead to the payoff of well-being: *an opening to freedom.*

There's a saying: *stop and smell the roses.* This is about taking time and taking note. Note the magnificence of the true miracle of what the seed has endured to become the beauty of the rose, and simply enjoy the nature of its becoming, the fruits of its labor. Nature exhibits its phenomenal capacities for realizing its potential through its similar patterns of design that work efficiently and effectively to naturally fulfill its purpose.

Nature knows the "code of conduct" guidelines that support a process to live and grow. For example, if you plant a seed, it will proceed on a natural course for its development. The order is present and does not have to be imposed from outside the system. Nature doesn't challenge the order, but instead goes with the flow and follows the inherent order. It demonstrates a perfect relationship. In doing so, it is fruitful under "ripeful" conditions. This activity displays one of nature's amazing secrets, akin to an instructional code within the tiny seed: *Given the right conditions, the seed takes the next step in creating what it is to become.*

It does so because it is a natural "calling," an order to follow for fulfilling its destiny to be what it is intended to become. There is no hesitancy in entering the darkness of the unknown. Nature knows that *the only way out is in* as it naturally seeks the higher ground to receive the light. It doesn't stay put, it moves forward and upward. It follows the order.

If you want to see a life in perfect shape, take a look at a nautilus sea shell. The nautilus, or spiraling seashell, presents an impressive example of natural living order. This aquatic wonder maintains its *proper authority* visible in its design that promotes its fulfillment of being a nautilus seashell. Its spiral shape adheres to a growing structure with a set of proportions that can be measured according to the Fibonacci series of mathematically precise dimensions. We see the same shape in galaxies, plants, and our own DNA.[20]

The spiral seashell and other living forms demonstrate the natural tendency to grow and develop in response to new information in the environment. The spiral seashell is a pleasing sight displaying alignment, balance, and consistency. Yet each is unique, and any part of it reflects the nature of the whole of itself. The nautilus seashell is an ordered whole, demonstrating its ability to remain *true to form*.

Who would argue nature is not successful in fulfilling its goals? For the human being, the application of these natural

---

[20] (Bernstein, 1998)

practices of order are the best kept secrets that can help us be our best as we proceed and progress with our lives.

Order in nature demonstrates recurring and timely activities that promote growth and change. The seasonal changes are one example of this. To have order in life means the same for the human as well. However, this is why change can be so hard. Why? Because what we establish as our customary mode of procedure, our habitual patterns of thinking and doing may not be in the best interest for our life's working order, and conflict with the *Law of Proper Authority*.

Inner conflict is a loss of order, a disorder of the self, as we lose our sense of well-being. We lose our form as we break the Law of Proper Authority. Hence, the apt descriptors of a conflicted person as being in "rare form" or "bent out of shape."

As anyone knows when seeing a posted sign that reads "Out of Order" it simply means it's not working. It's lost its proper authority of functioning. This then is what it means to be dysfunctional. You're out of order!

Perhaps the three most common words used by people in explaining their desires or justifying their behavior are: *"in order to…"* For example: "I did that *in order to* get this." It is a functional answer that implies there is a causal link between what we intend to do "in order to" achieve a certain result, or what we did through certain means that produced the ends. There is a right and proper working order to how our lives can proceed and progress in the higher interest of our well-being. The way we lead our lives and the direction we assume has much to do with the order we follow.

The Toilet Bowl Principle

Once when presenting a seminar on creating order in life, I introduced the topic by asking the audience if anyone knew what the "jiggle effect" was. One lady raised her arm and said

"I do."

"Oh? So what is the jiggle effect? I asked.

"This is the jiggle effect." She said, as she slapped the flab hanging under her raised arm. Well, it was an example of cause and effect, as her explanation of the jiggle effect caused instead a giggle effect! We all had a good laugh, but it wasn't quite the definition I had in mind. However, my answer was not as funny, since my head was in the toilet, so to speak. Let me explain.

The Jiggle Effect I am referring to is based on my Toilet Bowl Principle. If you've ever been in a bathroom and jiggled the handle on the toilet *in order* to get it to flush properly (function), you know what I mean by the jiggle effect (amazing where inspirational ideas can come to a person!) This jiggle effect represents an analogy for how we get a *faulty handle* on our problems and it means: *We work it out just enough to get us by only to have the same problem recur because we haven't addressed what's out of order on the inside.*

Flush-tration

Sometimes we do what gets us by, neglecting to do anything *on the inside* to address the part that's dysfunctional, and we overlook the out of order signs. We lose our order in life, and we are *not in service* to our True Self when the following "Out of Order" signs are posted within compromising our well-being:

- **WORN OUT PARTS:** We become absorbed in a part of our lives that dominates the whole of us. This is unnatural as any part cannot be greater than the whole.

- **OVERFLOW:** Too much coming in and not enough going out. We have taken on too much. Like a boat taking on more water than we can bail out, we're doomed to sink.

- **MISALIGNMENT**: Our actions do not support our values. Our goals are not aligned with our interests. We are out of line.

- **NOT PRESENT**: We fall back on the past or worry about the future in dealing with the present. We lose the life of the moment.

- **EMOTIONAL BREAKDOWN**: Our emotions take over and we come to believe the facts of life are the same as our feelings about life. If we're feeling bad, we may believe life is bad.

- **RESISTANCE**: We do not acknowledge what needs to be done and instead resist change. We see change as something being done to us.

- **BURNED OUT**: We lose our natural wellness as we become overwhelmed, stressed, and de-energized. We have little in reserve. We're running on empty. Cynicism and apathy begin to appear.

- **PAIN**: Pain is a signal from our body and/or an emotional state that requires maintenance. Its powerful message is: *"Now do I have your attention!?"*

What creates disorder for you? Are there signs of dysfunction you are ignoring? Check your vital signs of a different kind!

When you don't know what to do, you don't know how to act. As a result we can act out of fear and resistance. We're "acting out" simply because we don't know any better. As previously mentioned in the natural examples of the growing seed and the nautilus seashell, nature overlooks nothing, and is duty bound to the *order* of success factors and repetitive in a pattern of doing what works. These are natural habits of success.

Nature too has a way of expelling the parts that don't work as it is in constant movement toward the perfection of what it is to become. We, on the other hand, can instead be in constant movement toward satisfaction. What we find satisfying (tasteful and pleasurable) may not always be what's best for us. We are driven to satisfy our needs and desires and in doing so, we can create problems for ourselves as we negatively impact basic principles of healthy order in our lives. Now let's read some actions that will help keep us in order that follow and add meaning to the Law of Proper Authority:

1. **Stay In-formed**

    Remain open-minded. Information fertilizes our seeds of potentiality that grow new possibilities.

2. **Recognize Patterns and Implement the 5 Rs.**

    What you repeatedly do become patterns. Use the 5 Rs to identify and focus your change efforts for self-improvement and corrective action.

3. **Mind Your Ps (parts) and Qs (questions).**

   Return to your *personal why* to reaffirm what's important to you. Remember no part, or sum of the parts, can be greater than the whole of ourselves.

4. **Remember Your ABCs.**

   Create *Alignment*, maintain *Balance*, and practice *Consistency*. Our actions are aligned with our values in establishing meaningful life goals. A balanced life for a healthy whole of our lives can be achieved by staying true to form.

5. **Promote Cooperation.**

   Be a part of, not apart from. Inner work requires cooperative effort for efficiency and effectiveness for the greater good, a higher level of being and doing for a more ordered self.

6. **Re-Organize.**

   Make room for the new. Clean out the clutter in the mind. Simplify your life by throwing out worn out ideas and useless thoughts that no longer serve your purpose, or fit your lifestyle.

7. **"Inner-gize."**

   Give the rush a rest. Practice managing your "inner-gy." Keep your performance fuel tank *fulfilled* with mental clarity, emotional calm, and physical energy to drive your purpose.

When we focus on the natural tendency of order in life, we can be aware of adapting strategies to regain and sustain our proper course. Then you can relax and post the *in order* sign:

"Under new Self-management: Gone Fishing!"

Section II. Recap

Individuals with a mastery mindset seek challenging tasks and value learning because they want *to know and they want to act*. In this way they *stand firm*.

We can assume a proper authority over our mental activity with a firm basis from knowing more to do better, as we seek mastery over our lives. This authenticity of the True Self knows how to implement the right action.

Nature proves that a higher order of life already exists. It displays this order consistently, efficiently and productively. The cycles of nature illustrate this knowing and acting and life moves on. Our challenge is to place ourselves in unison and in compatibility with natural order. Then from the seemingly chaos of life emerges a way out of the maze as we access the powerful elements for creating order in life. As we step into the order, we step out of the chaos.

I remember in the Hidden Pictures how the images, through conscious effort and focused attention, just seemed to pop out of the chaos of the bigger picture. The hidden items emerged like magic to reveal themselves. We need to see the bigger picture for the order in the details of what we're in search of to assess whether they serve our purpose. We need to keep in mind our *P's* (the Parts) *and Q's* (the Questions) and ask the greater questions regarding the parts of ourselves that add to the whole of our life. Our bigger picture in life isn't chaotic when you've defined the details of what matters most to you. That's why it's the little things, and the simple that can make a difference.

Through order we find our way out of the maze and enter the amazing life as we leave the wandering behind and enter the wondering mind. We make headway as we clear the way in our head. If you want a practical example and its potential effect, try this with staff you supervise, or with any personal relationship: When a problem is presented to you, ask them for a solution. This creates the activity of "wondering" how to do rather than "wandering" around for what to do. Wondering is an essential thought process required for creativity. As we discover new firmament, a higher ground to take a stand on for *knowing and acting,* we then release our creativity to seek solutions rather than just identifying problems.

Key Points of Light

- Life naturally proceeds in a proper order.

- The Law of Proper Authority provides self-direction, respective of the natural order that supports an efficient and effective way of life.

- The answers to what you are looking for in the bigger picture we call life, lie within, but you must consciously seek them out by rising above.

- Patterns constitute a reliable sample of traits, acts, tendencies, and other observable characteristics of a person for insights into how one thinks and essentially how one lives.

- Pattern recognition is a valuable technique for not only identifying the details of our own life, but recognizing the ways of others.

- Our 5 Rs include our usual patterns found in our Routines, Responses, Requirements, Relationships, and our Reference.

- Flush-tration sets in when we do what gets us by, neglecting to do anything *on the inside* to address the part that's dysfunctional.

- The Toilet Bowl Principle results in flush-tration when we "jiggle" our *faulty handle* on a problem, only to have the same problem recur because we haven't attended to what's out of order on the inside.

- Be first with purpose in mind and do second when you answer to the greater questions of Why, and trust that the How will follow.

SECTION III.
Master Creativity

Creating Possibilities

In our increasingly complex, high tech world with a steady, more often an overflow, stream of information it is easy to get lost in the forest. One can lose sight of one's purpose simply by being overwhelmed with too much information. It can be distracting and often misleads us far away from what we desire to achieve. We lose our way.

As a living system, we seek sustenance for growth through an on-going process of filtrating information. We *think* our way through life, and then *do* a lifestyle. Our minds are constantly chomping at the bits of information as we feed the self to become the Self. This "human-essence" nature of the Self to be actualized has an insatiable appetite.

We feed our bodies through our minds as well. In fact, the word feedback implies this very process of thoughts circulating in our internal system.[21] It describes the critical human capacity to utilize information to create our lives. Just as we are what we eat, we are very much what we think. This means we are in-formed in the mode of processing information creating our lives. This becomes our "body of knowledge" for being somebody.

The wonder of creativity is the unexpected outcomes that create new possibilities. Creativity is stimulated by information. The more you know the more options emerge to "help yourself" in the act of making something new, including a new you. Know these acts of wonderment granted through the Master Key of Creativity that states:

All humans are inherently and spontaneously creative.

---

21 (Merriam-Webster, 2018)

CHAPTER EIGHT
FYI !

Be true to form

As lifelong learners, we learn our way through life. We, however, must not only learn to clear the air we breathe, but be open to receive what is vital for our lives as well as filter out the useless information. A balloon filled with too much air will burst but with the right amount will float freely higher and farther on its course. But to do so, we must release it. This metaphor offers an important secret for expanding ourselves to become a greater person and rise to a higher level:

We don't need all the air (information). We need only the right amount and what's right for us to realize the life we want to live. As we let in this expanding air and let go of what is no longer useful, we too will go higher and farther on our way as we release what keeps us tied downed.

Just like the life sustaining air you breathe, you should inhale the new and exhale the old. Be open to receive what is essential. Examine the following questions to help answer what may be stifling your creativity:

- What beliefs are no longer valid?

- What information acquired through a past experience, good or bad, does not apply to current events?
- What idea, once fresh, has passed its expiration date?
- What negative thoughts are creating negative results?
- What feelings are creating stress?

Dissipate the thoughts that no longer serve you and move them out of your system. This is more than thinking outside of the box, this is rising above the circle of self.

To Air is Human

Have you ever felt like a fish out of water? Only when a fish finds itself out of the water is the sudden realization of the importance of the water. Just like fish need water to live, we need information to thrive. But, we can drown in too much information.

Information works a lot like the air we breathe. Our physical being requires oxygen that serves as essential information for our bodies. Our bodies require the new life giving oxygen and releasing the old. This process represents the critical and natural physical act of *letting go*.

Every act of letting go was preceded by an act of grasping—the grasping of new information. Grasping what is essential to our lives, utilizing it for what it's worth, and letting go of what is unnecessary is critical to our well-being.

This illustrates the importance of remaining an open system continually processing the new, and then dissipating the old, spent information that no longer serves our purpose *in forming* (creating) the life we desire. In a nutshell (or a sea shell): *If you want a new life, don't hold your breath!*

Throw yourself back in the water! Be open to receive the new and replace what is no longer useful for your growth and well-being.

Clear the air and the water by asking: *What needs to be exhaled (letting go) for inhaling new life (moving on)?*

We see our way by receiving what is vital for our lives and discern what is useless information. Just like bad air, there is bad information. *To avoid the stale, you must inhale and exhale. To awaken and come alive, one must come up for air!*

There is no such thing as perfect information in the sense of knowing it all before acting, but how often do we react with little information? Most "know it alls" tend to do a whole lot of talking with very little walking. In other words they don't walk the talk! However, there is right information for right action. Here is a simple formula underlying all success, I call the *Up Right Principle:*

Right information for Right thinking creates Right actions for Right results. Right on!

An important corollary is to be assured: *There are a lot of right answers that are right for you.* Get yourself in the *upright* position and stand up for what's right for you. Stand high in your Truth!

Constructive Creativity

We build our lives one thought at a time and what emerges is the result of how we put them all together. We are a bit of a LEGO™ thought-set that provides the building blocks for different life constructs.

The wonder of creativity is the unexpected outcomes that create new possibilities. Creativity is stimulated by the process of self-awareness. The more you "know thyself" the greater possibilities emerge to "help yourself" in the act of making something new, including a new you. This creativity refers to the art of creating your life, and as unique individuals we can put our own twist on it.

Do you know about the Moebius strip? It's named after the German mathematician and astronomer Augustus Ferdinand Moebius who discovered it in 1858.[22] See it for

---

22 (von Oech, 1983)

yourself with the following activity: Take a strip of paper for the purpose of creating a loop. Before connecting the two ends, give one of them a half twist. Now tape the two ends together. Voila! There it is!

What there is may surprise you. Let's take a closer look with further demonstration. What you've created is a loop that now exhibits emerging characteristics, unexpected outcomes, and a new usefulness. This surprising *change of nature,* the result of putting a twist in the loop, is it now has only one side and one edge. You can prove this by drawing a line all the way around the loop. Your line will return to the starting point (all endings are new beginnings)! Yet, more amazing characteristics await. By taking a pair of scissors and cutting along the line you've drawn, you may think you'll cut it in half, but the result is not two separate loops, but unexpectedly, another Moebius loop twice as long! You've created something new that was there for the making, a new possibility, if only you knew about adding *the secret twist for creativity.*

The Moebius strip is an example of thinking differently, and how to engage creatively in order to discovery something new. Constructive creativity is life promoting (its opposite evil twin, destructive negativity, is self-defeating). Constructive creativity means we can build ourselves up by adding a "twist to our mind strip." This "twist" is possible when we recall our special creative capabilities to be:

- **Self-organizing**: We know the importance of order in our lives. Clean the clutter of your "work space in your mind" and clean the slate for new ideas to emerge.

- **Regenerating:** We can "rise again" demonstrating that from something old comes something new and every ending is a new beginning.

- **Resilient:** Resiliency is a skill acquired by the process of successfully "getting through it" and it breeds new ways of doing for success. Survivors can be unbelievably creative.

- **Connected:** See the connections of creativity and change as collaborators. We cannot have change without creation, and we cannot have creation without change.

- **Attractive:** What you project is what you will attract. Project a positive intention and receive the parts you need to make it so.

- **Instructional:** Our greatest attribute is our ability to learn how to live better. Learn something new.

- **Spontaneous:** Go ahead, jump in that rain puddle! Spontaneity promotes fun and playfulness. You don't plan spontaneity, it happens on its own in the Now.

- **Purpose driven:** Think of intention as invention. Your desires can become creations. Remember to ask the "Why" question and trust that the "How" will come.

Section III. Recap

Information fertilizes our seeds of potential that bears the ideas that create our lives. Just as we must open the window of a stuffy house to clear out the old and stagnant air, we must be open to allow the fresh air of information to flow through our minds. This is our window of opportunity for creativity that puts our best and fresh mind at the forefront.

We can induce creativity that provokes thoughts that evoke ideas. That's what's great about creativity— it loves to be probed and explored, thrives on questioning, and emerges with unexpected outcomes. Reclaim your inherent and spontaneous natural gift of creativity. Creativity is change and change is creativity. This means that we can create our own change.

Key Points of Light

- All humans are inherently and spontaneously creative.

- We don't need all the air (information), only the right amount and what's right for us to realize the life we want to live.

- As we let in the expanding air and let go of what is no longer useful, we too will go higher and farther on our way as we release what keeps us tied down.

- If you want a new life, don't hold your breath!

- To avoid the stale, you must inhale and exhale.

- What needs to be let go of (exhaled) for new life (inhaled) for moving on?

- To awaken and come alive, one must come up for air!

- We build our lives one thought at a time and what emerges is the result of how we put them all together.

- The wonder of creativity is the unexpected outcomes that create new possibilities.

SECTION IV.
Master Change

Being Change Ready

Long ago the Peruvian Indians saw the billowing, cloud-like sails of their Spanish invaders on the horizon. Having no concept of sailing ships in their limited experience, they believed it to be something related to the weather and went on about their daily living.[23] They assumed continuity, stability of tradition, screened out the fresh information that did not fit, and as a result were soon conquered.

There is one common thread that runs through change bothersome to most of us: It interferes with our natural desire for continuity in our lives. This common thread of change is more appropriately a common dread, messing with our personal patterns and it makes us uncomfortable. Our love of continuity can be a deceptive value because it can instill a false sense of certainty assuming predictability and security.

---
23 (Handy, 1990)

How do you feel about change? Is uncertainty challenging your sense of continuity? Is your norm threatened by the "abnormal?" Is insecurity invading? What "clouds" appear on your horizon? Change "disturbs" our continuity of the familiar when uncertainty sets sail, and on the horizon the unknown appears. Although most people struggle with change, we can be change ready when we accept the following life truth underlying the Master Key of Change:

We must change to live and live to change.

CHAPTER NINE
A New Change is in Order

Add venture to your life

We've all experienced those times of intense focus and heightened involvement in our actions. Those are the moments when life comes together perfectly and during that time all seems right in our world. There is unity and our effort flows without restraint. However, once we think about it, the experience is gone and we've changed the nature of it by introducing our thoughts. Mihaly Csikszentmihalyi, psychology professor and author, called such activity "flow." He characterized it as a "breakthrough to new levels of thought and behavior that occurs without social reinforcement and immediate rewards."[24] Basically, we do it because we like to do it. We get something out of what we get into. The motivation in doing is derived purely from the intrinsic value gained above any external benefits. Paradoxically, while nothing on the outside of yourself can make this happen, it occurs without the self, or at least the conditioned self that we know. It confirms an important secret regarding

---

24   (Csikszentmihalyl, 1990)

self-change: *The self that takes you in is not the self that will get you out.*

This notion means that *the only one that can change you is you,* yet the self that takes you into the change is not the self that will take you out as you emerge differently through the experience. A new change results in a new you. Or as Einstein put it: *"No problem can be solved from the same level of consciousness that created it."* [25]

The myth of change is you must hit rock bottom before you can climb back to the top. Change doesn't have to hurt and you don't have to hurt to change. Change neither picks you out or picks on you. It just is, and most of what "is" is what we make of it. We don't possess but *process* change, if we go with the flow. Although some, and I'm one of them, have a love hate relationship with change, we can be a master change agent.

The ART of Change

People value autonomy and self-determination. We generally want to call our own shots, love our freedom, and desire to make a difference. But to what extent do we believe we can affect the course of our lives? Perhaps the answer is found in the greater question that presents a challenge: *To what extent are you willing to venture into the unknown?*

---
25 (Albert Einstein: Brainy Quotes, 2020)

Of all life forms, only the human with our proper authority, can be self-directed. We have the option of choosing to be someone different and try something new. Why then, upon the realization there's another way to a better life, do we not jump at the opportunity to change? It's as if we have to be dragged, kicking, and screaming, all the way to happiness! Interestingly, we may choose to struggle, believing the survival mode is the only way to go. We may come to accept disorder as normal.

Why is there hesitancy, if not outright refusal to change for improvement? The answer is found in the following insight: *For most people, the thought of losing what they know or have (**continuity**), is stronger than their desire to discover something different (**change**) and therefore the unknown keeps us in our place (**fear**).*

This can make perfect sense. After all, being careful can be more appealing than risking an undesired result. This natural leanings toward the safe way has been proven in experiments confirming people prefer avoiding losses to acquiring equivalent gains.[26]

Hence, just the decision to have something different, to make the move out and up, is a difficult one. For better or worse, one may not like their current position in life, but choose to stay right where they are—the status

---

26   (Pinker, 1997)

quo. This is the so-called comfort zone. It is the *knowing about* our comfort that ties directly into our discomfort when the slightest disturbance can be threatening. I want the continuity of "sameness," so I resist anything that may change for fear of losing what I have. This is a common internal struggle between the comfort of the known versus the discontinuity presented by the unknown.

We know too well the common reasons that in reality are treasons for not engaging with a discontinuity presented by the unknown. These treasons betray the True Self from not going there, doing that, or going for it, like the following sample:

Risk averse: I don't want to lose what I have.

Lack of confidence: I don't have what it takes.

Low self-esteem: I'm not good enough.

Other directed: What would people say or think?

Outer directed: The current conditions don't allow it.

Inexperience: I've never done that before.

Unknown: I know nothing about that.

Losing: What if I fail?

Winning: What if I succeed?

Fear: Being afraid.

If you allow the False Self its treasons, one becomes exhausted before exhausting a list of "why we can't or won't" for proceeding out of the comfort zone.

Practice letting grow and moving on through the **A.R.T. of Change.** Remember the ART as an acronym to recall the critical elements within the process of change.

A—Abandon what was

- Acknowledging what you're holding on to that needs to go is the first step to letting go.

- Face yourself: Examine the "inner-fearance." What are your fears and resistance to change?

- Think versus thing: Can I separate and see the difference with who I am (my identity) from what I do (identifications)

R—Review your 5 Rs

1. **Routines**: How is this affecting my usual routines and habits?

2. **Response:** How am I reacting to the change? Can I respond differently?

3. **Requirements:** What does the change mean in terms of my requirements? Does it conflict with my preferences?

4. **Relationship:** How does it affect my relationships?

5. **Reference:** How does my past influence my perception of the present change?

T—Transition to the new

- Where are you in terms of giving up the old, and living up to the Now?

- How would you assess your attention, attitude, beliefs, emotions, and the will to let grow and move on?

Section IV. Recap

Something magic-like happens when self-change takes place, a sort of divine "inner-vention" that comes from within as you emerge differently. You experience a renewal as you shed the old self and a new you is born. It is like the alchemy of creating a golden moment out of a melding of ordinary ingredients transforming your life from the common and the same to something different. Who says you can't change lead into gold? Take the lead and change your life! Self-leadership occurs when you mix the right elements of your inner resources to create the valued life you desire. You come to know you are worth more than your weight in gold!

Higher principles for your transformation are at work and need nothing more than the usual, as they mix with the ordinary moments of the everyday living experience to produce extraordinary results. One of these higher principles is to rise above our usual self and we gain a new and strengthened being who is *doing*. We experience a sense of freedom, a tremendous power of will in self-direction, and welcome relief as we abandon our futile efforts to control anything outside of ourselves, and instead focus on our inner Self. We plug the psychic holes in the leaky bucket of the False Self that drains our inner resources by trying to control change. We join the natural movement of life in sync and in harmony. We go with the flow of the currency and the uncertainty. We make up our mind to *work with it rather than against it.*

Key Points of Light

- We must change to live and live to change.
- The self that takes you in is not the self that will get you out.

- Change doesn't have to hurt and you don't have to hurt to change.

- Change neither picks you out or picks on you. It just is, and most of what "is" is what we make of it.

- For most people, the thought of losing what they know or have (**continuity**), is stronger than their desire to discover something different (**change**) and therefore the unknown keeps us in our place (**fear**).

- There are common treasons that betray the True Self from not going there, doing that, or going for it.

- Practice the A.R.T. of Change by Abandoning what was, Review your 5 Rs, and make the Transition.

SECTION V.
Master Relationship

Cultivating Relationships

Auguste Rodin's famous sculpture, The Thinker, depicts a man perhaps battling with a powerful internal struggle. Besides a magnificent work of art, The Thinker provides a valuable insight into our physical and mental well-being, as stated in the following: *The body requires movement, but the mind requires stillness.*

Our body requires movement for good health and includes good stress upon our moving parts to function properly. While some of us may find physical exercise challenging, for most it is a greater challenge to keep our minds still. The reason is because it threatens our most important relationship: *The relationship we have with ourselves, and our self is the result of our thoughts.*

If we were given a penny for our thoughts, we would soon be rich. We have no shortage, but storage of thoughts, and we are challenged to take time out from thinking. We store our memories and thoughts of the days gone by of our experience. We carry our burdens that carry us away when we should carry on with life

The problem thinker is always under the influence of thoughts. It's a challenging practice *to get out of the know and be in the now.* The objective of meditation is to quiet the mind. It is the practice to experience peace, as we seek stillness from the chatter box of self talk. Wouldn't we stress less if our mind could take a rest? Wouldn't we experience a sense of tranquility if we would think less about what's bothering us? Wouldn't we relish the self-liberation from a life free of captivity, like birds released from a cage to live their purpose. Freedom at last from a mind filled with thoughts.

This is not thinking outside of the box but *being* outside of the box. It's an attempt to bring together all the moving parts, the "you haul" of thoughts, to realize the wholeness of simply being one, one with peace of mind. There is relief in the release of thoughts. There is rest for the weary thinker (and the mover). Detach the "you haul!" Unload the thoughts that weigh heavily on your mind, and move on.

Living a thought free life is, of course, impractical and impossible but this is not the objective. Remember, through developing our self-awareness for creating life success, we do have lofty goals that are ambitious, but attainable and realistic. A real alternative when it comes to mastery of our inner-world, is to choose not only what we think about, but how we think. This ability is our advantage and provides a valuable tool for realizing an improved higher self, a self that is aware, when we connect with our most important, yet challenging relationship—*the thought relationship*.

The Thinker's body language, gives the impression of *a whole lot of thinking going on, but not a thing moving on.* What then is he in relationship with that has brought him to a standstill? This masterpiece of art provides an example of how we can sculpt a new life through the Master Key of Relationship that states:

All is connected through relationship.

CHAPTER TEN
The Relationship Connection

Its not the thing, it's the think!

Thoughts can become "things." One of the most draining and dominating activities we can engage in is *too much thinking*. No wonder The Thinker rests his head on his hand, supporting a mind weighed heavily from thought and how apropos he's a statue, unable to make a move, suffering from the so-called "paralysis of analysis." Some mover, some shaker, and some thinker! I like the following story of the two monks and the woman that illustrates carrying the weight of burdensome thought.:

Two monks came to a river, which they had to cross. The river was flooded and there was no way that they would get across without getting wet. One lady was also at the banks of river, wanting to cross; she was weeping because she was afraid to cross on her own.

Since the lady also needed to get to the other bank, the older monk, carried her on his shoulders, and soon they reached the other bank, where he set her down. The lady went her way and the two monks continued their walk in silence. The younger monk was really upset, finding the other monk's act disturbing.

After a few hours the younger monk couldn't stand the thought of what had happened which kept filling his mind, and so he began to berate the other monk, saying, "We are not allowed to look at women, but you carried that woman!"

The other monk paused and with a smile on his lips he said, "I put her down when I crossed the river. Why are you still carrying her?"[27]

One thought can lead to another, just like connecting the dots to create a picture. We are cognitive beings and the content of our thoughts are so powerful they create the context of our lives. Hence, the most critical connection we maintain is the relationship we have with our thoughts as described in the following insight: *Any connection is a relationship, any relationship is a connection. Our connections create an energy flow. These connections can be enervating (life draining weak attractors) while others can be energizing (life giving strong attractors.)* Hence, an insightful question to ask yourself is: *What am I in relationship with?* Furthermore, is it the right relationship?

---

[27] (ahlhalau, 2020)

The bigger picture unfolds as you "connect the thoughts" from which the patterns of your lifestyle emerge. Connecting the thoughts becomes transparent as you see that it *isn't in the things, but the think*. The quality of relationship you have with others and things and how you think are one and the same. Hence, how you "inner-act" affects your interactions. Your inner work creates your external production as well as what you hold as your identifications as described in the following principle of "inner-action": *Our greatest time and effort (**attention**) is spent engaged in the thought relationship that creates in our minds who we <u>think</u> we are (**identifications**) and these thoughts become our standard operating procedures (**patterns**).*

We can assume our proper authority of leading our thoughts by understanding the thought process. We can utilize a law of physics and apply it to our psychic realm: *no two objects can occupy the same space*. Thoughts follow the same principle. You cannot harbor two thoughts at the same time. Thoughts enter our mind one at a time in single file, nicely in a row, yet ready to influence your mind to make some *thing* out of your thoughts. Their existence relies on the relationship you develop with them. In an instant, a thought can dominate by the act of *attention* and then quickly turn to *association* that attracts the next thought, and before we know it, a line of thought is created.

The Power of Negativity

Negative thoughts are weak attractors, yet strong, and are pushy. If negativity dominates our way of thinking, it is a destructive force to life, and wreaks havoc on our state of mind. What could have the moment been without a negative thought? What potential fell by the waste side as the result of negativity? It adds nothing of value to one's way of living and it stands in the way of a higher quality of life and happiness. It provides neither a solution nor long term relief from our problems. Dislike attracts only dislike and negative thoughts produce only negative results. Negative thoughts are like blackbirds perched in a row on a transmission line: *They tend to congregate, create interference, and can affect the communication signal.*

Here is a simple, but powerful, two-word sentence that holds great value to one's mental wellness and will help you shoo AWAY trouble-making thoughts: *Worries out!* The potential in this statement is two-fold. First, it means worry and negative thoughts serve no purpose, but to create mental unrest and some sleepless nights. Secondly, it recalls an important insight that our thoughts move, and you can consciously do AWAY (Acknowledge, Witness, Allow, and You're it!) with them. Ask yourself: *what would my life be like if I were to do AWAY with a worry that neither is or will be!* No worries! Imagine that.

When we shoo the blackbirds of negativity AWAY, we clear our line of thought for positive energy to flow as we resume connectivity to the True self. You can assume your proper authority as you lead your thoughts rather than being led by them. Your personal power is restored, or what may be called *empowerment*!

Identity Theft

Who was that masked man? Have you ever had the feeling that a part of yourself stole the whole of yourself?

We can become strongly connected to what we identify with. Someone can come to believe they are some *thing*. Whether it's a job position, a responsibility or role, a certain lifestyle, or even an opinion, we tend to identify ourselves by *things*. One can act as though these *identifiers* are a natural part of ourselves and be determined to hold on to these things. Hence, we defend what we depend on. It becomes self-defense because we fear if we lose them, we lose *the things* of ourselves. This is a mind game of the False Self that wants you to believe: *you are that thing*. It is a false notion that what we identify with is our identity. It is a case of mistaken identity.

Through our identifications, we label ourselves and others. Labels may be good for telling us what's inside a can of food (like Popeye's spinach) but they tell us nothing about what's inside a person (the content of the True Self.) You are not some *thing,* you are some *think;* and further, you are more and greater than you think you are!

Be aware that we are *self-taught through self-thought* as aptly stated as a matter of fact and a matter of warning by Ralph Waldo Emerson: "You become what you think about all day long."[28] Hence, good to know, not to just be aware but to beware!

We need to maintain a mind guard against identity theft. Let go of thoughts you hold that serve only to hold you back, keep you in your place, and limit your freedom to be, and to become. Letting go is an art, and a culinary art at that!

A Cooking Lesson in Letting Go!

In India, people catch monkeys with a simple jar of chickpeas. The monkey reaches into the jar to grab a fistful of their desirable treats. As the monkey clutches the chickpeas it cannot remove its fist from the jar rendering it helpless to fight back. The mouth of the jar is too small for its clenched fist and so the trap works because the monkey will not let go of what it is holding on to.[29]

---

28 (Ralph Waldo Emerson: Quoteslyfe, 2021)
29 (Goswami, 1993)

This same trap works on humans as well. Often people cannot resist the "cookie jar" that contains the desires, pursuits, possessions, relationships, and other valued gains. We get caught with our hands in the cookie jar as we reach for more and try to hold on to what we have. We experience the captivity by having our hands full. The result is we can't pull away long enough to enjoy the fruits of our labor. One can hardly savor the satisfaction of a job well done, or take time out to empty our hands (and our minds) from the activity of reaching for more.

A clenched fist requires more energy to maintain than an open hand. It is the same for our minds. An open mind requires less energy to sustain than a closed mind vigilant in maintaining what it has acquired, namely its history of experience, and one's beliefs. Despite the cookie jar that traps us and the proverbial carrot on the stick that we can never quite grasp, the life you desire is within reach by reaching within not to grasp, but *in order to let go.*

As a child, I learned an early lesson in the relief found in letting go from Don Cruz. Don Cruz was like a grandfather to me and lived next door to our house. He was my father's best friend and worked with my dad on the railroad. I enjoyed visiting Don Cruz because he was funny and entertaining with his antics.

One morning I watched Don Cruz prepare his breakfast. Unknowingly, my cooking lesson in letting go was about to be demonstrated. Don Cruz stoked the wood stove and placed upon it the metal skillet filled with refried beans. Then Don Cruz sat down at the table while they heated, and as I sipped on hot cocoa, my "Grandpa" began to doze off. It wasn't long before it was snores and smoke. Don Cruz' beans were burning!

"Don Cruz, Don Cruz. Wake up! Wake up!" I yelled. Don Cruz quickly snapped awake, but in a daze and in his haste, forgot the hot pad to pick up the metal skillet.

"Caramba!" he yelled, as he quickly let go of the hot handle, but then he reactively grabbed it up with the left hand only to get a second hurt. The result was a metal skillet filled with burnt beans served up on the floor. Ouch, and double ouch! Don Cruz suddenly became Don Cuss. I found the whole scene hilarious. Painfully funny, so to speak, was this lesson in letting go.

Looking back, I can't really say whether Don Cruz set up the whole scenario for my benefit of another funny show. Perhaps his intention, wise in his ways, was to show me a valuable lesson to awaken and come alive by letting go of the "hot handles" in life.

Section V. Recap

What's burning you up inside? What hot handle are you holding onto? Let go and spill the beans! They are the necessary losses by which you win the inner life. We can help ourselves without hurting ourselves. The self-help lessons we learn in childhood still apply. We can live a better life by letting go of the thoughts that are painful and hurtful. You don't need to hold on for dear life, but instead hold life dear. It is only when we gain the paradoxical new self-knowledge do we understand what it means to *make the connection to end the connection.* We must first see the attachment to make the detachment.

The most critical relationship to end is the relationship we have developed with self-punishing thoughts, life-wrecking emotions, and self-defeating behaviors. We surrender by giving up these debilitating thoughts that produce weak attractors that only work against us. Problems are to be handled, but often we seem to hang on to the hot pan longer, or let go of one only to pick up another. On the other hand, I'll try this, and ouch! We only get "burned" again. I know, I'll just "jiggle" the handle enough to get by with a temporary fix. Does the left hand know what the right hand is doing? Your solutions may then become the new problem! We may find ourselves, "here again" until we see the important connection through relationship: *To let go means to let learn, and to learn we must let go.*

Key Points of Light

- The body requires movement, but the mind requires stillness.

- All is connected through relationship.

- Our most important relationship is the one we have with ourselves, and our self is the result of our thoughts.

- Any connection is a relationship, any relationship is a connection.

- Our connections create an energy flow. These can be enervating (life draining weak attractors) while others can be energizing (life giving strong attractors.)

- Ask yourself: what would my life be like if I were to do AWAY with a worry that neither is or will be!

- Negative thoughts are like blackbirds perched in a row on a transmission line: They tend to congregate, create interference, and can affect the communication signal.

- Our greatest time and effort (**attention**) is spent engaged in the thought relationship that creates in our minds who we think we are (**identifications**) and these thoughts become our standard operating procedures (**patterns**).

- An open mind requires less energy to sustain than a closed mind vigilant in maintaining what it has acquired, namely its experience, and one's beliefs.

- The life you desire is within reach by reaching within not to grasp, but to let go.

CONCLUSION
Re-Tooling the Master Craftsman

Fire up! Stoke the coals of the aspire fire and get to work on forging your life with the right tools. A proverb states: "a good workman is only as good as his tools."[30] We have a mindset of power tools not only for surviving, but for thriving.

The real problem is we get used to doing things a certain way. We do as the psychologist Abraham Maslow stated: "If the only tool you have is a hammer, you tend to see every problem as a nail."[31] We attempt to solve our problems using the same response tool in every situation. Our solution can become our new problem because we're using the same ineffective tool and it doesn't work.

When we have in mind other tools for action, we still have a hammer, but no longer see every problem as a nail. We access a new mindset of power tools. We reach within to grasp the *right attitude, the focus of attention, the beliefs that cut through limitation, the emotions that affect our performance, and the will to do*. However, tools are useless

---

30   (Kinsella, 2021)
31   (Abraham Maslow: Quotes, 2021)

if we don't know how to use them in an effective way. "Know how" puts knowledge to work and it takes work to make a good living in every sense of the word. We learn through practical application as we hone these "knowing how" skills to create the life we desire to live. This "on the job training" serves as the inner instruction through our life lessons that cultivate a higher Self to grow with the proper use of these innate tools. All growth, which is movement, requires one essential first step:

Get Ready: *The willingness to leave the known.*

This then challenges us to make a sacrifice to…

Get Set: *The act of giving up one thing for the sake of another.*

This then presents the opportunity to…

Let Grow: *The choice to let go of old familiar patterns of thinking and behavior for something new.*

Through the practice of knowing thyself, we develop the "eyes to see and the ears to hear." We awaken and grow increasingly alert to our interior landscape to discover the hidden, to find what's meaningful and truly essential for a better life. As we *awaken*, we give up the fake as if stirred from a bad dream, and we *come alive* as we open our eyes to a new sense of Self for a higher life of being. Take a look at the following greater advantages as a result of the Self-study to know thyself :

- We become aware of our inner-life separate from the outer world.

- We know who we are and what we are not.

- We gain unity of the self rather than being fragmented.

- We receive what we are given rather than resist.

- We recognize our patterns of behavior.

- We learn to be watchful of the content of our emotions and alert in the context of our environment.

- We become conscious of our role in creating the quality of our living experience.

- We are more efficacious as we become more efficient and effective in fulfilling our intentions.

- We develop the skill of grasping what is worthy of our attention and letting go of the distractions.

- We develop new perceptions through new understanding and it changes our reality.

- We utilize a new mindset of tools and new possibilities emerge.

- We consciously promote the conditions to experience inner peace.
- We are comfortable with being ourselves as well as being with ourselves.
- We take responsibility for managing our thoughts.
- We come to know the True Self and the False self.
- We discover a higher level of life that is well worth the effort.

The more one discovers about oneself, the more challenges, perspectives, and opportunities unfold. We come to realize our guiding light of new understanding not only shows us the way but is an upward journey. We climb the mountain of self-realization to new heights of awareness, elevating us to higher levels of being. Just as sure as standing on a high mountain peak above all else, the view is much better up there!

This analogy of traversing an upward journey illustrates a simple but ancient principle required of all new and higher learning: *To see things differently a higher level of progression is necessary and is the result of leaving behind the lower level of thinking*. The higher vantage point becomes our advantage over the lower. Just as surely as the eagle can take flight, we have within us the power to *soar to new horizons!*

Along our journey we will fall, but with new understanding we are mindful to grasp the upper hand to help ourselves up. We dust off the particles of troubled thoughts, shake ourselves awake, and come alive! We look up, as we seek no other direction than to climb higher. We are upward bound!

References

Abraham Maslow: Quotes. (2021, January 21). Retrieved from Quotes: https://www.quotes.net/quotations/if%20the%20only%20tool%20you%20have%20is%20a%20hammer

ahlhalau. (2020, 11 20). *Two Monks and a Woman-A Zen Lesson*. Retrieved from KindSpring: http://www.kindspring.org/story/view.php?sid-63753

Albert Einstein: Brainy Quotes. (2020, September 25). Retrieved from Brainy Quotes: Https://www.brainyquote.com/quotes/albert_einstein_130982i

Bernstein, P. L. (1998). *Against the Gods The Remarkable Story of Risk*. New York, NY: John Wiley & Sons, Inc.

Blanchard, K., Hersey, P., & Johnson, D. E. (1988). *Management of Organizational Behavior*. Englewood Cliffs, New Jersey: Prentice-Hall, Inc.

Bridges, W. (1993). *Managing Transitions*. Reading, MA: Addison-Wesley.

C. S. Choules, Veteran of World War I, Dies at 110. (2011, May 5). Retrieved from New York Times: https://www.nytimes.com/2011/05/06/world/europe/06choules.html

Csikszentmihalyl, M. (1990). *Flow: The Psychology of Optimal Experience*. New York, NY: Harper & Row.

Encyclopedia.com. (2020, November 28). Retrieved from Encyclopedia.com: https://www.encyclopedia.com/science/encyclopedias-almanacs-transcripts-and-maps/archimedes-and-simple-machines-moved-world

Frankl, V. (2006). *Man's Search for Meaning.* Boston, MA: Beacon Press.

Ghyka, M. (1977). The Transmission of Geometrical Symbols and Plans. In M. Ghyka, *The Geometry of Art and Life* (pp. 111-112). New York, NY: Dover Publications, Inc.

Goleman, D. (1995). *Emotional Intelligence.* New York, NY: Bantam Doubleday Dell Publishing Group, Inc.

Goswami, A. (1993). *The Self-Aware Universe.* New York, NY: Jeremy P. Tarcher/Putnam.

Handy, C. (1990). *The Age of Unreason.* Boston, MA: Harvard Business School Press.

Hawkins, D. R. (2002). *Power vs. Force: The Hidden Determinates of Human Behavior.* Carlsbad, CA.: Hay House, Inc.

Howard, V. (1967). *Mystic Path to Cosmic Power.* West Nyack, NY: Parker Publishing Company, Inc.

Kinsella, J. (2021, January 20). *A workman is only as good as his tools.* Retrieved from Bible Prophecy Blog: https://www.bibleprophecyblog.com/2011/04/workman-is-only-as-good-as-his-tools.html

Merriam-Webster. (2018, June 26). Retrieved from Merriam Webster: https://www.merriam-webster.com/dictionary/feedback

Merriam-Webster. (2021, January 20). Retrieved from Merriam-Webster: https://www.merriam-webster.com/dictionary/attend

Murphy, M. R. (2002). *God and the Evolving Universe.* New York, NY: Jeremy P. Tarcher/Putnam.

New York Times. (2011, May 5). Retrieved from New York Times: https://www.nytimes.com/2011/05/06/world/europe/06choules.html

Order: Merriam Webster. (2020, July 19). Retrieved from Merriam-Webster: https://www.merriam-webster.com/dictionary/order

Patterson, M. R. (2011, February 28). *Frank Woodruff Buckles.* Retrieved from Arlington National Cemetary: http://arlingtoncemetery.net/fwbuckles.htm

Pink, D. H. (2009). *Drive.* New York, NY: Riverhead Books/Penguin Group.

Pinker, S. (1997). *How the Mind Works.* New York, NY: W.W. Norton & Compnay, Inc.

Plato: Brainy Quotes. (2021, January 20). Retrieved from Brainy Quotes website: https://www.brainyquote.com/quotes/plato_121792

Ralph Waldo Emerson: Quoteslyfe. (2021, January 20). Retrieved from Quoteslyfe: https://www.quoteslyfe.com/quote/you-become-what-you-think-about-all-4063

Reilly, L. (2011, March 12). *I'm no hero...I'm just a Marine*. Retrieved from Delco Times: https://www.delcotimes.com

Reninger, E. (2020, August 27). *History of Taoism through the Dynasties*. Retrieved from Learn Religions: learnreligions.com

Stark, M. (2008, August 8). *Deseret News*. Retrieved from Deseret News: http//www.deseretnews.com

von Oech, R. (1983). *A Whack On the Side of the Head: How to Unlock yur Mind for Innovation*. New York, NY: Warner Books, Inc.

CPSIA information can be obtained
at www.ICGtesting.com
Printed in the USA
BVHW082014121021
618753BV00001B/80